How to
Break Software
SECURITY

Effective Techniques for Security Testing

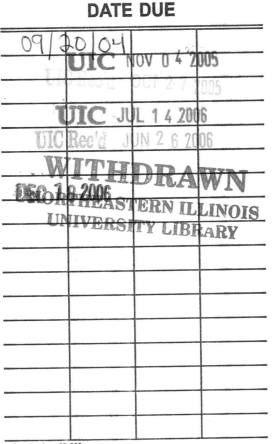

How to
Break Software
SECURITY

Effective Techniques for Security Testing

James A. Whittaker
Florida Institute of Technology

Herbert H. Thompson
Security Innovation

PEARSON

Addison
Wesley

Boston San Francisco New York
London Toronto Sydney Tokyo Singapore Madrid
Mexico City Munich Paris Cape Town Hong Kong Montreal

Senior Acquisitions Editor	Maite Suarez-Rivas
Editorial Assistant	Maria Campo
Marketing Manager	Nathan Schultz
Marketing Coordinator	Lesly Hershman
Production Supervisor	Marilyn Lloyd
Project Management	Keith Henry/Dartmouth Publishing
Composition and Art	Dartmouth Publishing
Copyeditor	Bryan Woodhouse
Proofreader	Barbara Passero
Indexer	Liz Cunningham
Text Design	Joyce Cosentino Wells
Cover Design	Joyce Cosentino Wells and Night & Day Design
Cover Image	© 2003 Jens Bonnke, Artville
Senior Manufacturing Buyer	Hugh Crawford

Access the latest information about Addison-Wesley titles from our World Wide Web site:
http://www.aw.com/cs

Library of Congress Cataloging-in-Publication Data

Whittaker, James A., 1965–
    How to break software security: effective techniques for security
    testing / James A. Whittaker, Herbert H. Thompson.
       p. cm.
    Includes bibliographical references and index.
    ISBN 0-321-19433-0
    1. Computer security. 2. Computer software—Testing. 3. Computer
    software—Reliability. I. Thompson, Herbert H. II. Title.

    QA76.9.A25 W48 2003
    005.8—dc21

                   2003048202

ISBN 0-321-19433-0   5/26/04
 2 3 4 5 6 7 8 9 10-HAM-06050403

Preface

About this Book

How to Break Software was the book that began the quest that this book, *How to Break Software Security,* continues. In the former book we treated the subject of software testing in a new and very practical fashion; the goal was to look at software and software bugs in a manner that made reasoning about bugs and finding bugs a more straightforward process. The idea was not to discuss theory but to show readers how to find real bugs in real software. The emphasis was on simple explanations and effective results. The intent of *this* book is exactly the same, except that our focus will be on a very specific and important class of software bugs: those that cause security vulnerabilities.

To be truthful, we never expected a book to emerge from our research into security bugs. Indeed, we expected that security bugs would be found using the same attacks that were published in *How to Break Software.* But that turned out not to be the case.

We discovered that security bugs have a life and habitat that defies many of the traditional testing techniques, even those presented in *How to Break Software.* The reasons behind this fact are presented in detail in this book, *How to Break Software Security.*

We began our research into security bugs after the Y2K scare was over. Y2K was a godsend for software testers. A mere mention of "date math" in a bug report circa 1999 would send any developer into a frenzy to fix the bug as fast as they could. Frankly, we got used to seeing our bugs fixed, and, well, we enjoyed it. When Y2K ended up being a nonevent, we were happy to find security vulnerabilities to be the next "holy grail" of software bug reporting. Security is to the twenty-first-century tester as Y2K was to the tester of the late twentieth century: a way to get bugs taken seriously.

But security is no Y2K scare. Security vulnerabilities are real and dangerous, and there is no magic date on which they will disappear for good. Security bugs are ignored only by the willfully ignorant.

Our research into security bugs began in a monumental fashion. The authors and a few chosen graduate students embarked on an analysis of every published security vulnerability that could be found; from bugnet to bugtraq to securityfocus.com to CERT advisories, we harvested them all. We basically reverse-engineered security bugs. We asked questions like: How was this bug discovered? What evidence could have been found that would have indicated that this bug existed? What testing technique would expose this bug? Our intent was to determine the root cause of each of these bugs and what could have been done to find them before the software was released.

We present the findings in this book in the spirit of the original *How to Break Software* book. We describe the general problem of software security from a tester's point of view, and then define very prescriptive techniques (which we call Attacks) that are designed to ferret out security vulnerabilities in software applications. As with the original, *How to Break Software Security* is intended to be easy to read and to provide readers with the techniques and advice they need to hunt down security bugs and see that they are fixed before the software they are embedded in is released.

You'll also find some interesting variations on familiar tools like Holodeck®, which shipped with the original *How to Break Software;* the version of Holodeck that ships with this book, however, is equipped with new capabilities for searching for evidence of security flaws. We've also included an easy-to-use port scanner that doesn't require a pocket protector to wield effectively.

About this Book's Audience

This book addresses one of the most critical issues in software today: security. The book has something to offer anyone involved in the development, testing, and use of software. That's a pretty bold statement, but the truth is that security affects everybody. The techniques described here are written for testers who may be new to security concerns, but these techniques also contain material that will be useful to experienced security testers and software developers. As the title implies, the book is written in a very "how to" style and offers practical testing guidance. Our initial intent was for this book to serve as a guide for students of testing and software engineering. It has evolved into a book that we think meets the needs of both students and software professionals to help build more secure software.

About this Book's Examples

In the original *How to Break Software* we showed screen captures of some pretty odd application behaviors. These "bugs" were meant to demonstrate how the techniques in that book were applied. In *this* book we address a much more sensitive subject, namely security vulnerabilities. By applying these techniques under contract with major software firms and government agencies, we've found bugs that leave applications wide open to assault by attackers. We present numerous examples in this book that illustrate our testing techniques. Some of these examples expose vulnerabilities in applications that reside on thousands and, in some cases, tens of thousands, of machines worldwide. For this reason, we use only previously published vulnerabilities—vulnerabilities that have been reported on public bug lists such as bugtraq and CERT.

About this Book's Organization

This book is organized into five sections. Part I, which contains only Chapter 1, describes the fault model that we use to guide security testing. In it, we discuss why security bugs usually evade traditional testing techniques and examine the mindset of a security tester.

Parts II and III present and discuss security "attacks" against software. These Parts contain Chapters 2, 3, 4, and 5 and detail tests that expose security holes in software. These chapters equip testers with the tools they need to identify design, implementation, and other software errors that leave the application, its host system, or user data vulnerable.

Part IV contains Chapter 6, the longest and most hands-on chapter in this book. In it, we examine three real software applications: Microsoft Media Player, the Mozilla Web browser (a free Internet browser), and OpenOffice.org (a freeware office application). For each of these applications, we run through the attacks of Parts II and III, and discuss how each of them can be applied. This chapter was born out of student and tester requests. It is designed to help testers who are given nothing but a binary to begin to test for security concerns. This chapter walks the reader through the process of identifying software risks and then conducting tests to expose security bugs.

Part V is the conclusion chapter. In it, we explain why security testing is a constant process, and why the industry is a long way from ever labeling a piece of software as "secure." It discusses how previous security bugs can inspire, though not direct, testing for future bugs, and offers some advice on implementing a security-testing program.

Also included at the end of this book are two appendixes. Appendix A presents a user guide for the Holodeck tool included on this book's CD-ROM. Appendix B is a reprint of an article from *IEEE Software Magazine* titled "Software's Invisible Users." We have included this article here, because it presents insights on the software-testing problem and on an application's interaction with its environment. Many application developers and testers think very narrowly about software input; they see only the GUI and think that it is the only entry point for delivering input to an application. The truth is that software receives input from many environmental sources, such as the file system, the operating-system kernel, and other software via API calls. This article makes this point and discusses a new model for thinking about software behavior.

About this Book's Supplements

This book comes with a CD-ROM that has tools and applications that will help you get the most out of the book. Two of the tools, Holodeck 1.3 and FITScanner, were written at Florida Tech. Those of you who have read the original *How to Break Software* will recognize Holodeck, an old friend enhanced with security features and now packed with more fault-injection and monitoring capabilities. Holodeck is the ultimate tool for monitoring an application's interaction with its environment and controlling the properties of that environment that an application sees. It allows tester's fine-grain control over failure scenarios at runtime, without ever having to modify a line of application code.

FITScanner is a new tool written by students at Florida Tech. It is a simple port scanner that testers can use to assess their application's exposure to the network. These tools are described in detail in Appendix A of this book

There are three applications that we target in Chapter 6: Microsoft Windows Media Player 9.0, Mozilla 1.2.1, and OpenOffice.org 1.0.2. We strongly encourage you to install these applications and use them to work through the examples in Chapter 6. Links to the tools and applications mentioned above can be found on this book's companion website: www.howtobreaksoftware.com/security.

Our hope is that we've continued in the tradition of *How to Break Software:* good advice that is easy to apply, with techniques that are sensible but novel.

Happy hunting!

James A. Whittaker and Herbert H. Thompson
Melbourne, Florida
2003

Acknowledgments

Although only two names appear on the cover of this book, the skill and techniques embodied within these pages are the result of the contributions of many people. The testers and developers that we have learned from over the years are too many to list, but we would like to acknowledge a few individuals who have selflessly invested their time and effort in discussing, editing, or reviewing the material in this book. Our sincerest thanks go to Dr. Mike Andrews, Scott Chase and Helayne Ray of Florida Tech; Terry Gillette of Security Innovation; and Ibrahim El-Far, David Ladd, George Stathakopoulos and Michael Howard of Microsoft for their many contributions to this book.

Our thanks also go to the Holodeck team, especially Terry Lentz of Florida Tech and Brian Shirey and Jason Taylor of Security Innovation. Thanks are due to Chin Dou who developed the FITScanner application that is included on the CD-ROM. Also, our sincerest appreciation goes to the book's reviewers: Kim W. Tracy of North Central College and Lucent Technologies; Timothy J. Shimeall of Carnegie Mellon University; Dr. Steven Atkin of IBM; Michael Howard with the Secure Windows Initiative at Microsoft Corporation; Yuliang Zheng of UNC Charlotte; Atif M. Memon of University of Maryland; and Scott D. Stoller of the State University of New York at Stony Brook.

Chapter Summaries

PART 1 INTRODUCTION

Chapter 1 A Fault Model for Software Security Testing

This chapter sets the stage for the rest of the book. It presents a model to help security testers conceptualize software's many sources of input and how security bugs can be hidden from traditional testing techniques. By taking the fault model to heart and examining software's interactions with its environment, we can be more effective at understanding security bugs and exposing them during testing.

PART 2 CREATING UNANTICIPATED SCENARIOS

Chapter 2 Attacking Software Dependencies

This chapter will help you attack software where it least expects it. Applications often rely on lots of external resources to behave securely. In this respect, most software development is done in a utopian environment, in which developer machines have plenty of RAM and hard-disk space, external files that are needed are always available, and the registry is a safe haven. This chapter describes ways of manipulating these resources, using Holodeck and other tools included on the accompanying CD, to replicate a hostile real-world environment. This is easy-to-implement, environmental fault injection at its best.

Chapter 3 Breaking Security Through the User Interface

This chapter gives very specific advice on what to do when you are in front of the keyboard, mouse in hand, looking for a series of clicks or keystrokes to uncover interesting behavior in the software you're testing. It covers attacks that are delivered to the software the way developers thought they would be—that is, via the command window, text fields, buttons, etc. Here we offer guidance on crafting these inputs in ways developers and designers may not have anticipated, compromising both the application and its data.

PART 3 DESIGN AND IMPLEMENTATION ATTACKS

Chapter 4 Attacking Design

Designing secure software is a complex task. Software architects and developers often overlook the implications a design choice has on the security of the application and the system that executes it. This chapter offers attacks that give testers the ability to weed out some common design problems from their application.

Chapter 5 Attacking Implementation

Even if the design of an application is secure, there are lots of bad things that can happen when specific implementation choices and errors are made. This chapter presents techniques for exposing some common implementation vulnerabilities using attacks from the user interface, combined with behind-the-scenes information and manipulation.

PART 4 APPLYING THE ATTACKS

Chapter 6 Putting It all Together

This chapter gets down to real hands-on work and shows how the attacks of Chapters 2 through 5 apply to real applications. It takes a close look at three applications: Windows Media Player and the Mozilla web browser on the Windows platform and OpenOffice.org for Linux. It walks through each application, discusses how to assess the security threats to that application, then shows and discusses how the attacks presented can be applied to that application.

PART 5 CONCLUSION

Chapter 7 Some Parting Advice

This chapter discusses where we think security testing is headed. It also shares some lessons learned from our own security-testing experiences and talks about pitfalls and how to avoid them.

APPENDIXES

Appendix A Using the Tools on the Accompanying CD

This appendix provides user guides to the testing tools included with this book, the most important of which is Holodeck. Holodeck is a tool that allows testers to observe and control interactions between an application and its environment. It lifts the veil of an application and lets us see what's really happening behind the scenes by bringing interactions between the application and its "hidden users" (such as the file system and the OS) to the foreground. More importantly, it lets us intercept these transactions and control them to simulate a wide variety of environments that would be difficult to produce otherwise in the test lab.

Appendix B Software's Invisible Users

This appendix is a paper that originally appeared in *IEEE Software Magazine.* We include it here because it offers an interesting perspective on software and its interaction with not just the human user, but with software and hardware users, as well. Several of the attacks in this book operate under this view. It also gives a better perspective on how tools that apply and manipulate inputs from these hidden interfaces fit into the overall testing picture.

Annotated Glossary of Terms

If you should happen to overhear a conversation between security gurus, you might hear terms like *disassemblers, script kiddies,* and other colorful phrases that often seemingly have nothing to do with software. The Glossary defines and explains the common software-security terms as well as terms used in software development and testing in general.

Table of Contents

PART 1

Introduction

0011001011011000110 100

CHAPTER 1
A Fault Model for Software Security Testing

A **fault model** is a way of thinking about how and why software fails. Fault models for software are numerous and address everything from process maturity to programming-language constructs and software behavior. *How to Break Software* [1] introduced a behavior-based fault model for software. The idea behind the fault model was to understand problematic software behaviors, so that testers could more easily plan and execute effective tests designed to exercise software to look for defects. This chapter specializes that model to specifically address software failures that have security implications. We are exclusively interested in faulty software behavior that results in security compromises. The model came about through painstaking analysis of thousands of published security vulnerabilities and of vulnerabilities that the authors and their team found in released software. It is designed to help testers understand how security vulnerabilities are created and to give insight into how to better find them. In later chapters, the fault model will be refined into specific, prescriptive testing techniques that we call "attacks."

Why Security Testing is Different

Software testing is the discipline of executing a software application to determine whether it meets its requirements and specifications. When software behaviors are found that fall outside of required or specified behavior, we say that the software failed because of one or more embedded defects (more commonly called faults or bugs).

One might think that this definition would subsume security testing, because it seems obvious that no one would actually require or specify insecure behavior. Thus one could argue that traditional testing should be equipped to detect security bugs. Indeed, in a perfect world with perfect specifications and a flawless understanding of security implications, this would no doubt be true. But specs aren't perfect, and security requirements are very poorly understood. Therefore, it is an important exercise to study the difference between security vulnerabilities and traditional bugs and to begin the process of refining our testing strategies so that they are better equipped to expose bugs that have security implications.

There are two main tools that testers use to locate and diagnose traditional bugs. First, there are techniques that allow testers to think through the selection of input scenarios that are likely to force the software to fail. Second, there are symptoms of software failure that testers are taught to look for in order to know when an application has failed. These two topics are covered at length in the first book in this series, titled *How to Break Software* [1].

Unfortunately, the truth is that security vulnerabilities do not fit the standard description of software bugs. Not only do many of the standard techniques for selecting input scenarios miss important security concerns, but also the symptoms of security vulnerabilities are very different from those of traditional bugs. This book addresses these differences by first analyzing the nature of security flaws and then developing practical techniques to locate and diagnose security-class software bugs.

In the spirit of the original book, this book begins by describing a fault model for software security in order to put security testing into the context of software behavior. This will give us insight into the problems that security testing poses and some initial understanding of the potential solutions that we must devise to address this very difficult problem. This fault model is the subject of this chapter.

Subsequent chapters will then expand the lessons of the fault model into specific attacks that are aimed at breaking software in ways that expose security vulnerabilities. Once again, we will rely on a few cool tools to make our lives as testers easier. Readers of the original book will find a familiar tool called Holodeck® on the companion CD. However, this version of Holodeck is equipped with some new features that will help carry out some of the more vicious security attacks. Also included on the CD is a port scanner that we built with testers in mind. It is not a typical port scanner that only registered geeks can use but rather a scanner built *by* testers *for* testers that can quickly and easily expose open port risks.

Security is the biggest modern software development and testing problem faced by the professional development community. This book will explore the tools and techniques that are necessary to ensure that security concerns are well tested, making the software you build more secure.

What is Software Security?

Security concerns are different for any given application.

Some software publishers are concerned with **piracy** of their application, in whole or in part. They want to sell their application to every user and not have it copied illegally and sold on the black market. To these publishers, security means keeping their binaries safe from illegal copying.

Some publishers present their software for free but only allow access to certain parts of the application to registered users. These publishers are interested in ensuring that every user gets only the access they paid for and are thus concerned about **access control.** They want everyone to have their software, but they want only authorized users to be able to access the parts that they paid for.

Some publishers are concerned about their application's vulnerability to malicious input. Publishers of server applications that listen to network ports or desktop applications that execute mobile code are particularly worried about **buffer overruns** and malicious use. These publishers are intent on ensuring that their applications cannot damage local resources or cause malicious code to execute.

Other software publishers are worried about the data that their software processes. The data must remain secret for all but authorized users. These publishers must worry about data being stored in plain text or data that has a predictable pattern of residence in memory. Their concern is to keep their data secret.

Indeed, there are many concerns that software publishers have. Thus any bug that causes a CERT advisory[1] or has the potential to cause harm must be considered a security vulnerability.

A Fault Model for Security Vulnerabilities

Software can be *correct* without being *secure*. Indeed, software can meet every requirement and perform every specified action flawlessly yet still be exploited by a malicious user. This is because security bugs are different from traditional bugs. In order to locate security bugs, testers have to think differently too.

---

[1]CERT is a major reporting center for Internet security problems. They are most well known for their *CERT Advisories* which alert users to newly discovered security vulnerabilities and threats.

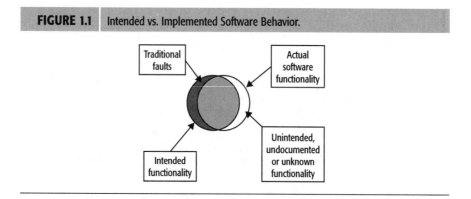

FIGURE 1.1 Intended vs. Implemented Software Behavior.

Consider Fig. 1.1, which shows two overlapping circles. The first circle represents the software's intended, perfect behavior. The second circle represents the actual behavior as coded into the product by developers. As you might expect, these two circles rarely, if ever, overlap perfectly; that is, the software executes its intended functions—and *only* its intended functions—as it was designed to.

The intersection of the two circles represents the behaviors that are correct and secure. This part of the software, shown in light gray in the figure, is the intersection of intended and actual functionality—that is, the behaviors that were coded exactly as intended, without insecure side effects. Obviously, the larger this intersection, the better and more secure the software.

The left part of the figure, shown in dark gray, is the portion of the software's intended behavior that never got implemented or that was implemented with deficient functionality. It is here that we find most traditional software bugs: behaviors that should work one way but are either incompletely or incorrectly implemented. This type of buggy behavior is familiar territory for testers and the focus of my previous book, *How to Break Software.*

The right part of the figure shows the portion of the software's actual behavior that is *not* part of its intended behavior. In other words, rather than not executing correctly the functions it was designed to perform (that is, traditional software bugs), the software does extra things that it is not supposed to do. It is in this area that many security vulnerabilities exist. The problem here is that the behaviors that are not supposed to happen are often masked by the fact that the software also satisfied its requirements.

These additional behaviors are called *side effects,* and they represent the biggest threat to software security.

Imagine a web server that is supposed to accept http requests from port 80 but that also sometimes manages to overrun buffers by not checking for maliciously crafted packets. Simply observing behavior will not detect the overrun, and the fact that the software *appears* to function correctly masks the buffer overrun from scrutiny.

Imagine a media player that flawlessly plays any form of digital audio or video but that does so by writing the files out to unencrypted temporary storage. This is a side effect that software pirates will be all too ready to exploit.

We see from this fault model that security deficiencies are quite different from the functional bugs we are used to finding. Traditional bugs are found by looking for behaviors that don't work as specified. Security bugs are found by ignoring the specifications and looking instead at additional behaviors, their side effects, and the implications of interactions between the software and its environment. The next section discusses how security bugs fit into a more familiar software testing paradigm.

Security Concerns and the *How to Break Software* Fault Model

Software security is like any other type of physical security; it means keeping secrets. A secure application is an application whose secrets are as safe as possible. Most secrets that an application possesses—such as passwords, encryption keys, private user data, and so forth—must be both stored internally and occasionally transmitted to its environment. Indeed, what good is information if it can't eventually be used for its intended purpose by its intended users? The key to security is to keep the information from *unintended* uses by *unauthorized* agents.

Thus it is useful to consider software's environment as a potential place in which security can be breached. Moreover, it is also useful to look inside an application where secrets are kept and test internal security as well. A useful way of thinking about software's internal computation and environment interaction is the fault model presented in *How to Break Software*.

FIGURE 1.2 The fault model presented in *How to Break Software.*

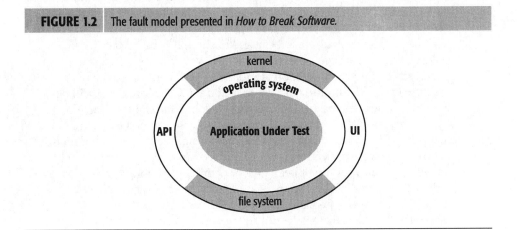

Fig. 1.2 shows this model of a software system [2] (see Appendix B for a more thorough description of the model). This fault model describes the extent of software security concerns because such concerns generally

relate to the software causing insecure side-effect behaviors that are detectable (and exploitable) via components in the software's environment. As shown in the figure, there are four classes of users for software: the **operating-system kernel** provides memory, file pointers, and various services, such as time and date functions; the **file system** provides data stored in either binary or text format; the **user interface** is implemented as a set of APIs that get inputs from the keyboard, the mouse, and other devices; and, finally, other **software** systems (APIs, databases, runtime libraries, etc.) can supply inputs and data as return values of API calls.

The security concerns for each of these users are presented in the following discussion.

Security and the User Interface

User input consists of inputs that originate from a user interface (graphical, command line, or menu-driven) or inputs that arrive through an application's API (in which case the "user" is a program). Security concerns from these interfaces include unauthorized access and sabotage. Furthermore, we are interested in malicious input because user-interface inputs often have a counterpart in remote input. Thus security concerns visible through the UI can also indicate that vulnerabilities exist that may be triggered by remote users as well.

The first testing consideration for the human user interface is access control, which is usually implemented via password protection and user authentication. The problem here is to ensure that unauthorized access is improbable and, perhaps, to test that weak passwords or authentication risks are minimized.

After a user has been authenticated, there still may be access controls to consider. Indeed, rarely are all users treated in the same way. Some users have access to more data and functionality than other users, and the controls that implement this access must be tested.

After access controls have been established, it is important to understand, via testing, the extent to which important internal data is accessible. If your application is processing critical, secure data, you should test the limits of access to that data. Certainly there will be legitimate ways for authorized users to view or transmit this data, but it is a tester's job to determine all possible access methods to secure data, including copy/paste, screen captures, and other ways in which data can be taken from an application without authorization. Determining what secrets an application must keep and how an application guards those secrets from unauthorized users is an integral part of security testing.

Finally, an area of consideration already covered in *How to Break Software* is that of malicious input. Any crashes of an application, particularly buffer overruns associated with long string attacks, must be taken seriously. A crash through the user interface is a bug that might also be triggered through a network interface. A crash is a crash, and it represents denial of service or, in the case of the buffer overrun (which will be covered in depth in subsequent chapters), potential execution of malicious code instructions .

Security and the File-System User

Interaction between an application and the file system is usually untested and often left to chance by testers. Security testers cannot afford to be so lax. It is often the case that the file system is entrusted to store sensitive data, passwords, and other such persistent information. We must be able to test the way in which this data is stored, retrieved, encrypted, and managed for security. Imagine an application that stores information about itself in the Windows registry or some other form of central data storage. If a malicious user figures out that, for example, license information is stored in the registry, then we've just handed them the keys to our application. Software pirates are ready to undercut software producers; there is no reason to make their job any easier. If testers are aware of how such license information is stored, then they may be able to expose piracy opportunities long before illegal copies can be made.

Security and the Operating-System User

Any information that an application uses must pass through memory at one time or another. Information that passes through memory in an encrypted form is generally safe, but if it is decrypted and stored even momentarily in memory then it is at risk of being read by hackers. Encryption keys, CD keys, passwords, and other sensitive information must eventually be used in an unencrypted form, and their exposure in memory needs to be protected.

Another concern with respect to the operating system is stress testing for low memory and other faulty operating conditions that may cause an application to crash. An application's tolerance to environmental stress can prevent both denial of service and situations in which the application may crash before it completes some important task, such as encrypting passwords. After an application crashes, it can no longer be responsible for the state of stored data. If that data is sensitive, then security may be compromised.

Security and the Software User

It is important to remember that most applications rely heavily on other software and operating-system resources to perform their required function. Thus our application is only as secure as the other software that it uses. We must therefore build a catalog of external components that our software makes use of, and test the interaction that can occur along these interfaces. If our software reads information from a network port, then we must worry about invalid and ill-formed packets, overly long or short packet frames, and other such interface-specific concerns.

Another security concern, when dealing with component software environments, is the dependencies that naturally exist between software components. (Mutual reliance is necessary, but mutual trust should not be taken for granted.) Components that your application depends on can fail, crash, or even be compromised in some way that may affect your own component's security.

Security must be a team effort among component software (and even hardware), and breaches can occur when any component is compromised. If the remaining components are unaware of the breach, then they are just as much at risk as the component that allowed the intrusion in the first place.

Testing software and the software it relies on to accomplish its mission means having a global view of the environment in which the software is operating. This means understanding each software interface and interdependency and knowing how to test these interfaces for potential security vulnerabilities.

Security Inside the Software

Sometimes it is the software itself that must be protected. Many applications have proprietary algorithms or optimizations that give them an edge over competitors, and these secrets need to remain secret. The art of learning these secrets from a compiled binary is called **reverse engineering.**

Reverse engineering is a painstaking and difficult endeavor made easier (but still not *easy*) by tools called **disassemblers.** In essence, a hacker will use a disassembler to convert an executable binary file, which only computers can understand[2], into a more understandable format. Think of them as the reverse of a compiler. A compiler takes a programming language that is understandable by humans and converts it into machine language (binary code) that is executable by a computer. A disassembler reverses a binary and produces information understandable by humans (although they do not produce source code).

Creating an Attack Plan

At first glance, it seems that we could organize a plan of attack by looking at each method of input delivery individually, and then bombarding that interface with test input. For the original *How to Break Software* book, this is exactly what we did. There we found that test cases that involved only a single input source found bugs—lots of bugs. The most severe security bugs, however, usually don't manifest through a single input source. We found that the most revealing security attacks require us to apply inputs through multiple interfaces. With this in mind, we set out to determine what types of tests are likely to uncover security vulnerabilities in soft-

---

[2] The authors are aware of some people who claim to be able to read binary code. However, it is unlikely that such people would ever find it productive to do so. Disassemblers are much faster and more effective at interpreting binary code, and even people capable of such manual disassembly would likely employ such a tool to make their job easier.

ware. In our quest we pored over thousands of security bugs and incident reports and for each one asked the following questions:

- *What fault would have caused this vulnerability?* In some cases, we had access to source code and could determine the fault categorically. In other cases, we had to infer what we thought to be the most likely set of faults that would be capable of causing such behavior. In this way, we gained insight into the root cause of many software security faults.

- *What were the failure symptoms that would alert a tester to the presence of the vulnerability?* Because we studied security vulnerabilities in released software products, we surmised that either the failure symptoms were unobserved by the original testers, or the causal fault was never executed. In either event, we thought it of paramount importance to understand exactly what faulty behaviors we needed to be on the lookout for when we performed our own security testing. Indeed, what good is a test case without the ability to correctly identify symptoms of failure?

- *What testing technique would find this vulnerability?* This is the ultimate question for security testers: exactly how do we go about testing for security vulnerabilities? It wasn't surprising to us to discover that for many of the vulnerabilities, no existing testing technique could have readily uncovered them. Thus we created many new testing techniques, or attacks, that would enable us to find the vulnerabilities in the software under test.

The result was a set of techniques, some old but most new, designed to uncover security bugs in software. We applied these techniques over and over again under the aegis of testing contracts from both corporations and government agencies. Over the years, we have honed these techniques and developed an arsenal of "attacks" that has proven effective at exposing security vulnerabilities on every software product we have come up against. The result is this book.

The attacks fall into four broad categories: software-dependency attacks, user-interface attacks, attacks against the application's design, and attacks against the implementation of that design. We have dedicated one chapter to each of these four attack classes. The following is a brief description of each of the four chapters:

Attacking Software Dependencies

Gone are the days when software merely relied on a few operating-system resources to function. Modern software is a complex meld of third-party libraries, interconnected components, complex operating-system routines, and hardware. Most applications do not handle failures of these resources in a secure manner. Consider, for example, a Web-enabled application that writes out sensitive transaction information to a file if the network connection fails or an application that relies on an external library to supply some security service but fails to check whether that library loads properly.

   Chapter 2 presents testing techniques to help ensure that environmental failures do not expose the application or its data to an attacker. Those of you who have read the original *How to Break Software* book will see a familiar tool to aid in simulating common environmental failures: Holodeck. In this book we have included a more feature-rich version of Holodeck, which has the ability to both monitor an application's interaction with the environment and also simulate a larger number of environmental failures.

User-Interface Attacks

Buffer overflows are by far the most publicized and feared vulnerabilities in modern software. Every year, buffer overflows and other user-input exploitable vulnerabilities cost the software industry billions of dollars. Although the dangers of unconstrained input are well known, applications still routinely fail to validate data supplied by users. Chapter 3 focuses on exposing data-dependent insecurities in software. This includes attacks to uncover buffer overflows and input-validation problems with escape characters, commands, and alternate character sets.

Attacking Design

Many security vulnerabilities may be designed into the application from the beginning. Obviously, no ethical or prudent development organization would ever do this intentionally, but it is often very difficult to foresee the impact of high-level design decisions on the security of an application or its host system. Test instrumentation is one example of this. It is common for test instrumentation to be designed into an application from the beginning, so that automation harnesses and other testing tools can efficiently execute tests. In a lot of ways, test instrumentation is a necessary evil; it's necessary to meet testing goals, but it also tends to inextricably interweave itself with the functional code of the application. The result is that many applications ship with test instrumentation. This occurs either because some application features have become dependent on it or because long-abandoned testing hooks are forgotten in the frenzy of development modifications leading up to the release of the application. Additional application "features" such as this can give attackers a clear and often unimpeded entry point into the application, its host system, or user data. There may be other serious design problems as well, and Chapter 4 presents attacks that expose many of these security-related design flaws.

Attacking Implementation

Even if an application's design is secure, implementation decisions and errors can still leave the application vulnerable. Consider a typical large development organization working on a complex application. In such a situation development is often very compartmentalized; that is, a developer is given a small component to write that fits in with other components that all come together to create the functioning application.

Developers may get detailed definitions about which interfaces their component should expose and the precise form of the data entering and exiting that component. They are also likely to receive functional requirements of how that component should process data internally. These functional requirements are usually well communicated, and indeed they must be in order to create a working application. The problem is that developers are usually only given a very small piece of the overall picture. They may not be aware, for example, that the data their component receives is sensitive and should not be written out temporarily to the file system. Many times miscommunication such as this leads to severe application vulnerabilities. Chapter 5 confronts this problem and presents attacks that have proven successful in exposing implementation-related vulnerabilities.

In keeping with the tradition of the original *How to Break Software* book, we have organized testing techniques into **attacks.** Each attack is a stand-alone, focused testing technique designed to uncover security vulnerabilities. For some interfaces you will need specialized tools to apply the desired inputs. All the necessary tools are included on the accompanying CD-ROM, and they will be discussed throughout the book as well as Appendix A.

Conclusion

Security concerns surround testers. Every software interface can harbor opportunities to compromise sensitive information that must be guarded against. When an application fails to guard this information properly, many dire consequences can arise. It is the job of testers to ensure that every safeguard is implemented properly and that security is as good as it can be.

However, security can never be absolute, and testers will never be able to anticipate every opportunity that a hacker might have to obtain sensitive information. Awareness of the problem's scope and a diligent effort to test each interface for exposures is the best way to instill confidence in an application's ability to execute securely in an insecure world.

Exercises

Professional testers can try these exercises on whatever application they are currently working with. We encourage students to try these exercises on an application they use frequently. This will give you a good warm-up to the attacks that follow. When we train new security testers, we like to go through all the exercises twice: once on an application that the student knows well and uses often and then again on an application they have never used before. The exercises force the tester to look at new applications from a security perspective.

After you've picked your application, work through the following:

1. Why do most functionality tests miss security vulnerabilities?

2. What are the four classes of software users? Give an example of each application user.

    a. For each class of users, list some potential security concerns relative to your application.

3. Take ten minutes and list sensitive data that your application either processes or uses (passwords, CD keys, etc.).

4. Name the four classes of software attacks.

    a. Take ten minutes and list as many of your application's dependencies as you can think of. Think about libraries, files your application reads, etc.

    b. What kind of input does your application take through its user interfaces? Does it process strings from the user?

References

1. J. A. Whittaker, *How to Break Software: A Practical Guide to Testing.* Boston, MA: Addison-Wesley, 2002.

2. J. A. Whittaker, "Software's Invisible Users," *IEEE Software,* Vol. 18, No. 3, pp. 84–88, May/June 2001.

PART 2

Creating
Unanticipated
Scenarios

CHAPTER 2
Attacking Software Dependencies

011001011011000 1 100

Applications rely heavily on their environment in order to work properly. They depend on the OS (operating system) to provide resources like memory and disk space; they rely on the file system to read and write data; they use structures such as the Windows Registry to store and retrieve information; the list goes on and on. These resources all provide input to the software—not as overtly as the human user does—but input nonetheless. Like any input, if the software receives a value outside of its expected range, it can fail.

In the past, creating these environment-induced failure scenarios was difficult. It required us to force specific code paths to be artificially executed. This approach isn't very feasible in the real world because of the amount of time, effort, and expertise it takes to artificially force just one failure in the environment. Even if we did decide to use a code-based approach, the problem is determining where in the code the application uses these resources and how to make the appropriate changes to simulate a real failure in the environment.

The answer to most of these problems is implemented as a tool called Holodeck, which is included on the accompanying CD-ROM (See Appendix A). Holodeck allows us to watch an application interacting with its environment and to control responses from the environment to the application. This information can give clues to how and when the application uses these resources. Based on this information, we can launch our attacks and selectively deny application resources.

Environmental Fault Injection

This chapter discusses simulating failures in the application's environment, a process known as **environmental fault injection.** When extraordinary conditions occur because of stress and the failure of

(continued)

(continued)
dependencies, error-handling routines, if present, are executed. These are pathways through the application that do not add to its functionality but are designed to keep the functional code from failing. Error-handling routines though are notoriously subjected to far less testing than the functional code that they are designed to protect. They are underrepresented because in the past causing environmental faults has meant modifying the application's code directly and hard-coding bogus return values. To compound the problem, many failure situations are not envisioned during the design stage, and error handlers are added as afterthoughts as vulnerability situations are encountered in the test lab.

With such limited exposure to testing, these code paths are fertile breeding grounds for bugs. Software can only be considered secure if it operates securely in all reasonable operating environments. Thus to have any realistic picture of an application's security vulnerabilities, it must be exposed to environmental failures.

There are three basic approaches to simulating environmental failures in a lab situation:

1. **Source-Based Fault Injection:** Source-based fault injection can be complicated to achieve but is easy to explain: source statements are modified so that specific faulty behavior is attained. When faults are injected to trigger exceptions, source statements are added, so that internal data can be set to values that cause exception conditions to evaluate to true. However, source-based fault injection requires access to source code and, in most cases, the cooperation of the original developers, which is not always given.

2. **Runtime Fault Injection:** Applications access external resources through function calls to the operating system, such as requesting memory, disk space etc. Runtime fault injection involves getting between the application and the OS and intercepting these calls. This ability is embedded in the Holodeck tool included on the CD-ROM that came with this book. Using these techniques, we can control responses from system calls and selectively deny resources such as memory, disk space, files, libraries, etc.

Many attacks in this chapter use runtime fault injection techniques as the primary means for introducing environmental failures into the system. Using Holodeck, you will be able to simulate these environmental failures to ensure that your application behaves securely when failures in the environment occur.

| **ATTACK 1** | Block access to libraries |

WHEN to apply this attack

Software depends on libraries from the operating system, third-party vendors, and components bundled with the application. This first attack is designed to ensure that the application under test does not behave insecurely if software libraries fail to load. As testers, it is our responsibility to ensure that such failures do not compromise security. The types of libraries to target depends on your application. Sometimes DLLs (Dynamic Link Libraries) have obscure names that give little clue to what they're used for. Others, as you will see below, can give you hints to what services they perform for the application. You may need to consult documentation that describes the services performed by every library or external resource that your application loads.

WHAT faults make this attack successful?

Developers tend to take the success of system and library calls for granted. This assumption can be dangerous, because applications often rely on library code for validation routines. If these calls can't be executed or return unexpected errors, the application might not have appropriate error handlers in place to respond securely.

When environmental failures like these occur, application error handlers get executed. However, sometimes these situations are not considered during application design, and the result is the dreaded unhandled exception. Even if there is code to handle these types of errors, this code is a fertile breeding ground for bugs, because it is likely that it was subjected to far less testing than the rest of the application. In the discussion following, we will show how Holodeck can be used to easily simulate these faults and put such code through better testing scrutiny.

HOW to determine whether security is compromised

Dependency failures can take many different forms. The application may just crash. If this happens, it's likely that there was no code written to handle the failed library call. Although this may be an important bug, it's less interesting to the security tester than some other possible outcomes. A full-scale crash though may still cause sensitive data, such as passwords or other application-protected secrets, to be "dumped" out to the screen or to a file that might be worthy of investigation.

A more interesting reaction to dependency failure occurs when the application appears to continue to run properly even though a library failed to load. Failure of a library to load deprives the application of some functionality it expected to use. An application that does not react to this failure by displaying an error message or crashing is a sign that appropriate checks are not in place. The underlying problem is that return values from library loads are often not checked. This means that features that try to use these resources may attempt to use data and functionality from the library without first checking return codes. The results can vary from data corruption to the application failing to perform some critical validation task.

HOW to conduct this attack

The first step in conducting this attack is to find out which libraries your application accesses and when. This is where Holodeck comes in. You can exercise the application under Holodeck and monitor the library operations. In Windows, LoadLibrary is the key function here. The first argument in "LoadLibraryExW"[1] holds the name of the library the application is trying to load. By observing these values, you can determine when the application loads which libraries and plan your attack. Sometimes the filename itself can give you a clue to which functions it performs for the application; if not, consult the documentation of the library or discuss its functionality with the developer.

A good example of a suspicious library load can be found in Microsoft's Internet Explorer (IE) web browser. Figure 2.1 shows Holodeck in action, monitoring IE for calls to the "LoadLibraryExW" function. The astute security tester will notice the ominously named file "msrating.dll."

You may be familiar with IE's "Content Advisor" feature that allows, say, parents to set a password to block certain web sites. Testers familiar with this feature will immediately become suspicious of the "msrating.dll" library and what might happen if it failed to load. We'll execute our attack to find out.

First, let's look at what IE's (Internet Explorer) content advisor feature is intended to do. If you turn the feature on, by default, all web sites that don't have a RASCi[2] rating are blocked. Figure 2.2 shows the message displayed by IE when we try to navigate to an unrated site with Content Advisor enabled. If an incorrect password is entered, an error message pops up, and we can't get to the blocked site. If we click cancel, we still can't get to the site, which means Content Advisor is working as intended. Now let's see what happens when we *don't* allow IE to load our suspicious dll.

---

[1] LoadLibraryExW is the Unicode version of the Windows LoadLibrary function used with Microsoft Windows 2000 and later versions.

[2] The Recreational Software Advisory Council (RASCi) rating is assigned to a Website based on its content. This rating system was replaced in 1999, however, with the Internet Content Rating Association (ICRA) rating system.

FIGURE 2.1   *Holodeck* monitoring library loads in Internet Explorer.

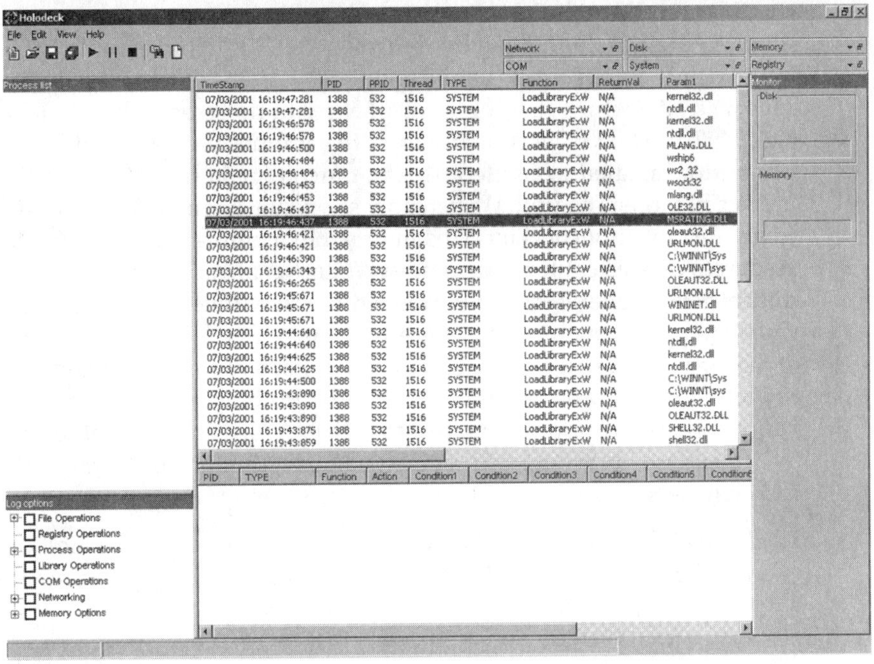

FIGURE 2.2   Internet Explorer's® Content Advisor feature blocking access to an unrated site.

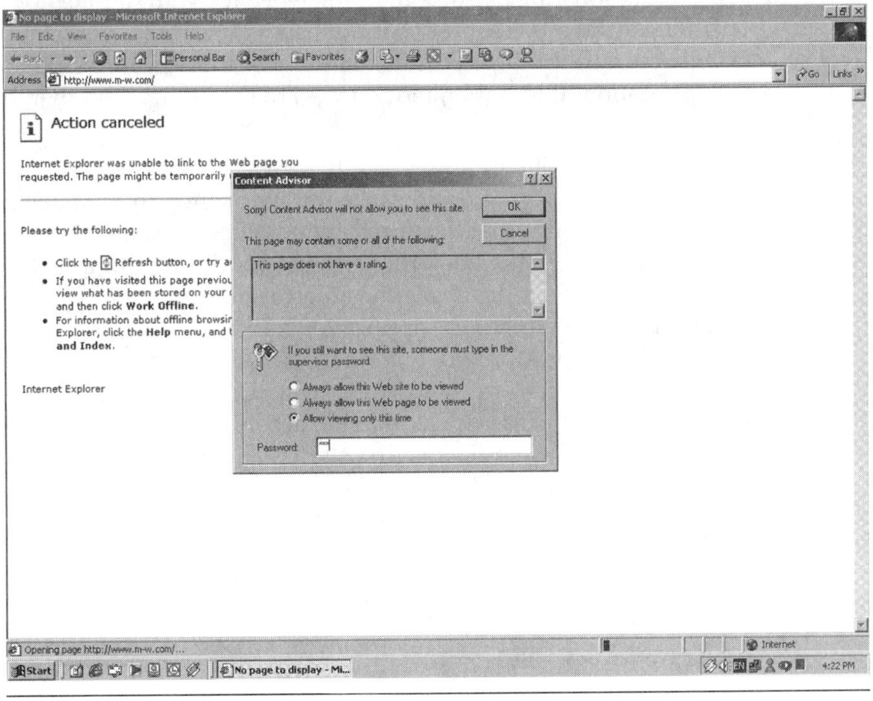

Using Holodeck's Predefine Tasks option, we select the LoadLibraryExW function to be intercepted as shown in Fig. 2.3. We ask Holodeck to look for all such calls with the string "msrating.dll" as the first parameter and simulate a failure in this call by returning "NULL"[3] to the application; then we launch IE in Holodeck's environment. We next try to navigate to a blocked site, which IE happily displays with no error! Take a look at Fig. 2.4. This shows the content tab of IE's options window; notice that the two buttons related to Content Advisor are grayed out.

What happened here? We can only speculate, but a likely scenario is that when Content Advisor is invoked, Internet Explorer replaces the functions used to fetch Web content by functions found in msrating.dll, which perform content-related checks. When we denied IE that privilege, it failed to check whether appropriate functions were actually replaced. This is a good example of this first attack succeeding. By failing the LoadLibrary command, the security rating feature was completely negated. This is an example of an insecure failure mode of an application. As security testers, we must hunt these down.

To expose library-related security failures, think through the following steps:

1. Note all libraries used. Holodeck is key here; you can use Holodeck to watch library loads and note which actions are being performed by the application when the load request is made.

2. Try to reason about which libraries identified in step 1 might impact security. Look for names that are suspicious—that is, similar to our msrating.dll library. You should be armed with a list of libraries from the application's specifications or documentation from previous versions of the software. Also, a good reference for your application's operating system is essential. For libraries you can't identify, talk to developers and try to determine the services those libraries extend to the application. If in doubt, block access to the library, and then begin testing for insecure behavior.

3. Block access to a library and watch for insecure behavior. Most of the time, a failed library load will cause the application to crash. During a crash, the concern is that the application may leave the system or user data in an unsafe state. Look for sensitive data being dumped to a file. A failed library load causing an error message or an application crash is a good sign that the application attempted to carry out its tasks without the features provided by the library. Try to determine which tasks the application was performing when it tried to load the library in question. In our Internet Explorer example, the library msrating.dll was loaded both when IE was first started and again when we enabled the Content Advisor feature. A little detective work will expose which features fail to function because of a failed library load and the implications this has for the application's security.

---

[3]NULL is a special value that indicates there is no value. As the return value of a function call, NULL usually indicates failure.

FIGURE 2.3   Holodeck blocking calls to LoadLibraryExW when it tries to load msrating.dll.

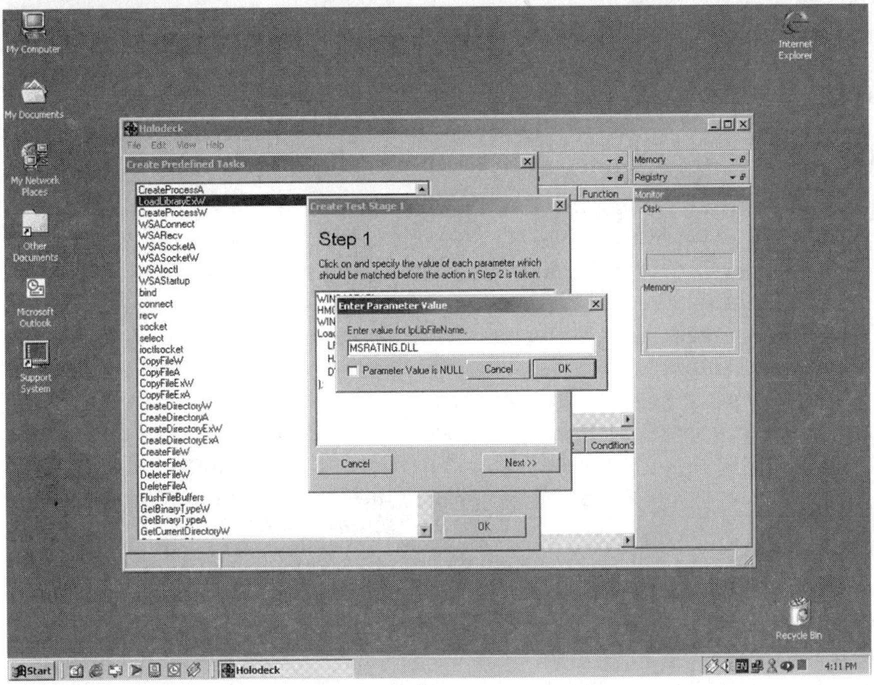

FIGURE 2.4   If msrating.dll is not loaded, the buttons for Content Advisor are disabled, and no error message is raised.

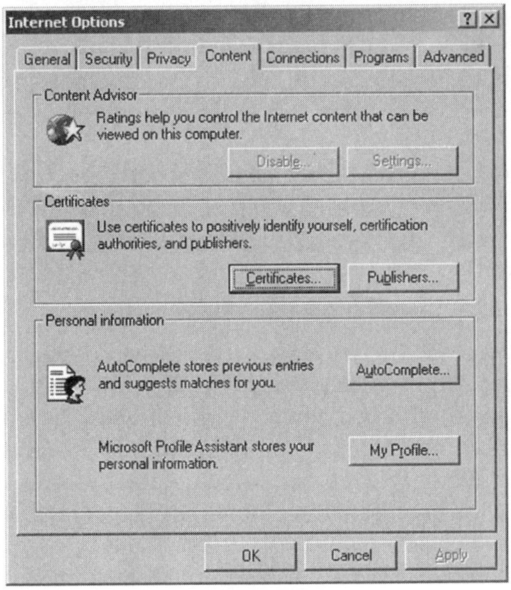

ATTACK 2   Manipulate the application's registry values

The Windows registry is a database used to catalog the resources used by the Windows 95, 98, NT, XP, and Server 2003 operating systems. It replaces the Win.ini, Autoexec.bat, Config.sys, and System.ini files used in Windows 3.1x (although Windows 95 and Windows 98 maintain these files for use with older software). Whenever a user makes changes to Control Panel settings, File Associations, System Policies, or installed software, the changes are reflected and stored in the registry.

The physical files that make up the registry are stored differently, depending on your version of Windows. Under Windows 95 and 98, the registry is contained in two hidden files in your Windows directory, called USER.DAT and SYSTEM.DAT; for Windows ME there is an additional CLASSES.DAT file, whereas in Windows NT/2000 the files are contained separately in the \System32\Config subdirectory of the system directory.

WHEN to apply this attack

In the Windows world, the registry contains information crucial to the normal operation of the operating system and installed applications. For the OS, the registry keeps track of information like key file locations, directory structure, execution paths, and library version numbers. Applications rely on this and other information stored in the registry to work properly. However, not all information stored in the registry is secured from either users or other installed applications. This attack tests that applications do not store sensitive information in the registry or trust the registry to always behave predictably.

Testers can apply this attack whenever a registry key is read or written by the application. The attack can be applied directly by using a registry editor to manually alter values or on the fly with Holodeck.

WHAT faults make this attack successful?

The problem with the registry is trust. When developers read information from the registry, they may trust that the values are accurate and haven't been tampered with maliciously. This is especially true if their code wrote those values to the registry in the first place. This attitude can lead to big security problems. Never assume that data you read was created by you.

One of the most severe vulnerabilities occurs when sensitive data is stored unprotected in the registry. This could be as simple as plaintext passwords or user-access information. More complex information stored in the registry can cause problems, too. Take, for example "try-and-buy" software, in which users have either limited functionality or a time limit in which to try the software, buy it, or both. In these cases, the application can then be "unlocked" if it's purchased or registered. In some cases, the check an application makes to see whether the user has purchased a legitimate copy is to read a registry key at startup. We've found that in some of the best cases this key is protected with weak encryption; in some of the worst, it's a simple text value: 1 indicates a full-capability, purchased version; 0 indicates a trial version.

This attack attempts to expose such faults, which may lead to the piracy, theft, or availability of sensitive data.

HOW to determine whether security is compromised

In some cases, just reading the registry keys an application writes can compromise security. For plaintext passwords, the vulnerability is obvious, but this is only the beginning. User-access information, clues to implementation, confidential user information, and clues on how to get it are all inappropriate uses of the registry.

For vulnerabilities that can be exploited by changing these registry values, it is important for testers to be aware of which features and data would normally be available to the user and which should be restricted. The next step is to watch the application after it reads the altered registry values and try to see what is restricted, what isn't restricted, and what application behavior may have changed. In some cases, it may be necessary to restart the application to see results, especially for try-and-buy software.

HOW to conduct this attack

The first step is to find registry keys that the application relies on. Holodeck can be a great resource here. By watching the application as it executes, we can see registry reads and writes when they happen. Particularly interesting times are during installation, at application startup, when updates are installed, when passwords are changed, when users or resources are authenticated, and when the application is shut down. We can first be a passive observer, looking at which information the application is using from the registry, what is being written out, and how this data could be used to extract unintended information. Once critical registry dependencies have been found, the next step is to start altering values and observe how the application responds.

One option for changing values is to alter them on their way to the application. Again, Holodeck can be used to intercept the system calls an application makes to read and manipulate the registry; using it, we can manipulate these values nonintrusively. Another option is to change the values directly. In both the home and business incarnations of Microsoft Windows, registry values can be manipulated using Regedit, a tool shipped with the OS. Regedit requires administrative rights on the machine to view, add, or change many registry keys. The truth, though, is that in a typical organization, lots of users have administrative rights to their local machine; in fact, many of these machines have standard administrator passwords. Also, many viruses use vulnerabilities in network applications that run as "System" and have control over the registry. An obvious argument here is that if a malicious user has administrative rights on the machine, all bets on security are off anyway. For the most part that's true, but in the case of many try-and-buy applications discussed above, the entire business model of a company precariously depends on *no one* changing these values. There are also many other cases in which this is true, as we will see in the following example.

Let's take a look at UpdateExpert, a utility sold by St. Bernard software to manage updates and patches of critical applications. From their website,[4] we learn, "UpdateExpert is a Windows administration program that helps you secure your systems by remotely managing service packs and hotfixes. Microsoft® constantly releases updates for the OS and mission-critical applications, which fix security vulnerabilities and system-stability problems. UpdateExpert supports Windows NT, 2000, and XP, and a long list of mission-critical applications."

FIGURE 2.5   Holodeck monitors for registry interactions.

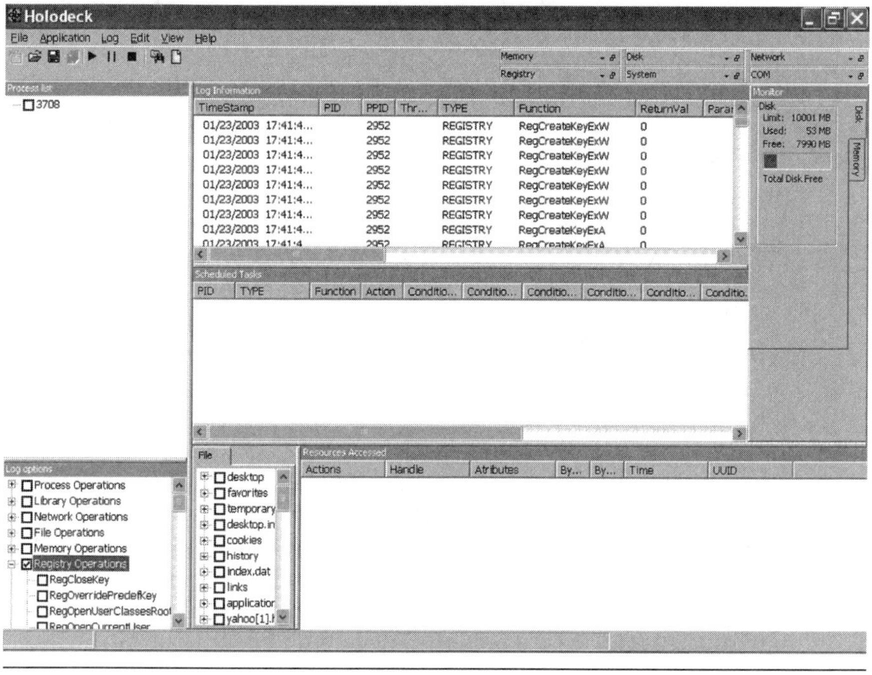

---

[4]www.updateexpert.com

FIGURE 2.6 UpdateExpert shows an installed patch on the local machine.

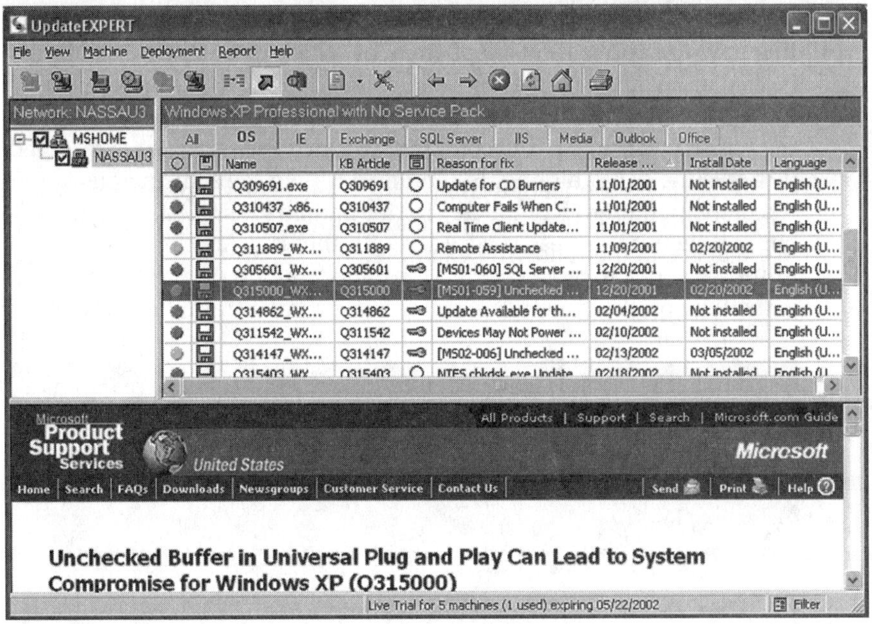

FIGURE 2.7 Windows stores information about installed patches in the registry. The key "Installed" tells the application that a patch has been applied.

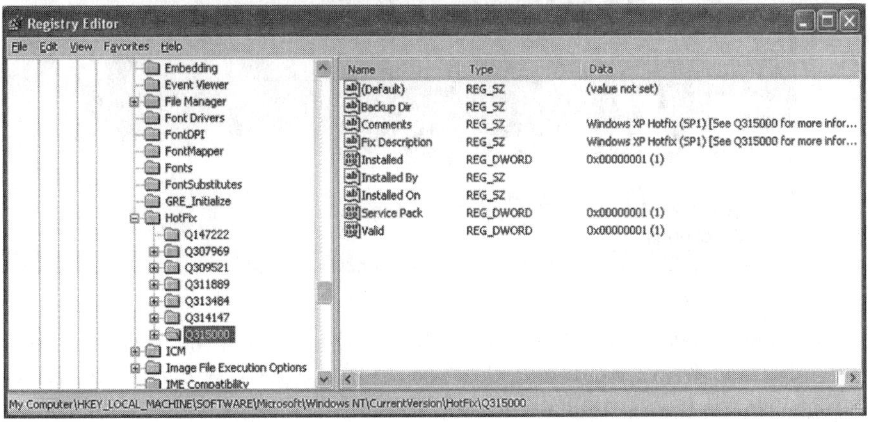

For this attack, we first launch the trial version of UpdateExpert under Holodeck and watch for registry operations. Figure 2.5 shows that when we click on the local machine within UpdateExpert (Fig. 2.6), the application reads the path

```
hkey_local_machine\software\Microsoft\Windows NT\
CurrentVersion\Hotfix\
```

from the registry. The alert security tester would then ask the question "Is this how the application keeps track of which updates are installed?" Notice in Fig. 2.6 that there is a field called "KB Article" in the OS tab. You will notice that these values appear to be very similar to folders stored in the registry in Fig. 2.7. By examining a patch that actually is installed—in this case the patch highlighted in Fig. 2.6—we see a suspicious key under the corresponding "KB Article" folder named "installed." What would happen then if we created a folder with the "KB Article" number of an uninstalled patch and added an "installed" key with the same value? This is the type of question that security testers must train themselves to ask.

FIGURE 2.8	An alert tester would ask the question, "Can we fool the application into thinking an uninstalled patch, like the one highlighted here, is actually installed?"

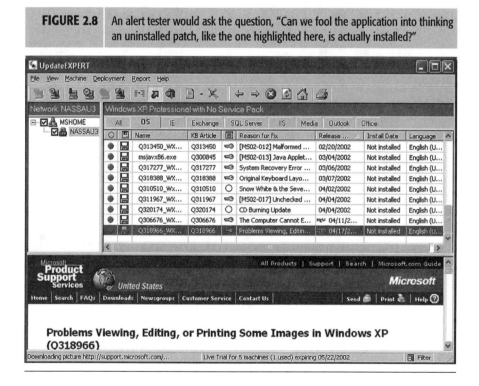

Take a close look at Fig. 2.8. Highlighted is a patch that has not been applied with KB number Q318966. In the registry, we now create a folder with the key "installed" set to 1, as shown in Fig. 2.9. If we then restart UpdateExpert, Fig. 2.10 shows the patch as installed!

This product apparently uses the registry to record which updates have been applied to applications and the operating system[5]. For this par-

---

[5]This issue was originally reported on NTBugtraq (www.ntbugtraq.com).

ticular type of application, relying solely on the registry for this information is not advisable, because someone with access can fake the installation of a critical security patch by simply altering a value. In the worst case, as shown here, UpdateExpert can show system administrators that all released security patches have been applied; meanwhile, a malicious insider can exploit supposedly fixed vulnerabilities in the system remotely.

FIGURE 2.9	We create a folder with the same name as an uninstalled patch's KB article number, and in that folder create an "Installed" key with value 1.

FIGURE 2.10	UpdateExpert reads our bogus registry directory and key and now indicates that the uninstalled patch is installed.

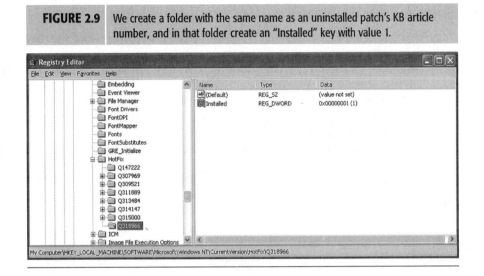

ATTACK 3 | Force the application to use corrupt files

WHEN to apply this attack

Software can only do so much before it needs to store or read persistent data. Data is the fuel that drives an application, so sooner or later all applications will have to interact with the file system. Corrupt files or file names are like putting sugar in your car's gas tank; if you don't catch it before you start the car, the damage may be unavoidable. It's our job as testers to make sure that our applications can handle bad data gracefully, without exposing sensitive information or allowing insecure behavior.

A large application may read from and write to hundreds of files in the process of carrying out its prescribed tasks. Take a look, for example, at Microsoft Word or Internet Explorer under Holodeck. Files are being read from and written to almost continuously. Every file that an application reads provides input; any of these files can be a potential point of failure and thus a good starting point for an attack. Particularly interesting files to check are those that are used exclusively by the application and not intended for the user to read or alter; they are files where it is least likely that appropriate checks on data integrity will be implemented.

WHAT faults make this attack successful?

It is the application's responsibility to check that data is in an acceptable form before it is used. Developers are usually pretty good at this for user inputs. GUI (Graphic User Interface) input fields may have a forced length limit, checks might be made to ensure that numerical inputs are actually numbers, and fields that contain required data are usually screened. Indeed, user input is perhaps the best-constrained class of inputs to an application.

When it comes to the file system, though, checks are usually not as thorough, because most testing done in practice is through the user interface. The conventional thinking here is that if the application is going to get "bad" data, user input is likely to be the most common source.

In addition to bad data, another source of file-related problems is the application's checking of file names. This is a common—and sometimes spectacular—cause of failure of an application. In our experience, error checking for file names is even less common than the checking of file contents. It's the first contact an application has with a file and is thus usually accepted without checking the value for escape characters, length, etc. The example shown later in this attack description demonstrates what can happen if appropriate checks are not in place.

HOW to determine whether security is compromised

Many potential breakdowns in security may be exposed by this attack. Probably the most obvious and common is denial of service, which happens when the application takes in bad data and chokes on it. This is especially true of server applications that accept files from remote users. The symptoms in this case are pretty obvious: the application reads a bad file and promptly dies. Other common, though less obvious, failures (such as data corruption) can occur at this point, as well.

Note that a crash that results from a corrupt file may be a buffer overrun. If this is the case, the impact of the failure can be much more severe than mere denial of service. If an attacker can get the file to be read on a target system, they can execute arbitrary commands on that machine.

Another sign of potential security failure is corrupt data being displayed on the screen. Although corrupt screen data is unlikely to be a security failure, it is a sign that input-validation routines can be bypassed and bad data can make its way into the application. The next step is to try to isolate the source of that data in the file and then apply the input-string attacks of Chapter 3 to expose potential insecurities.

HOW to conduct this attack

This attack is carried out by identifying a file that the application will use and changing it in some way that the software may not have anticipated. For instance, for a file that contains a series of numerical data that the software reads, we may want to use a text editor and include letters and special characters. If successful, this attack usually results in denial of service by either crashing the application or bringing down the entire system. More creative changes may force the application to expose data during a crash that the user would not normally have access to. When searching for buffer overflows through file data, we have also found random file corruption to be very effective.

Let's take a look at a specific example of this attack. You may already be familiar with Eudora®, a popular email client. Among other features, Eudora allows users to send and receive email messages and also acts as a viewer and editor for these messages. In this example, we attack Eudora Pro Version 4.01 by altering an email message before it is retrieved from the server. Specifically, we create a message with an attachment that has a very long file name[6]—in this case, 300 characters. Why 300? Well, many operating systems and clients that send mail allow a maximum file-name length of around 200 characters. In Windows, this value is usually MAX_PATH, or 260 characters. Other mail programs though are not bound by this constraint, so such an email may be sent directly from one of these clients, but it's something testers may not have thought about.

---

[6]This bug was originally reported on bugtraq at http://online.securityfocus.com/archive/1/60175.

FIGURE 2.11   We can manually corrupt the header of an email–in this case with a long attachment name–and then send it directly through the Simple Mail Transfer Protocol.

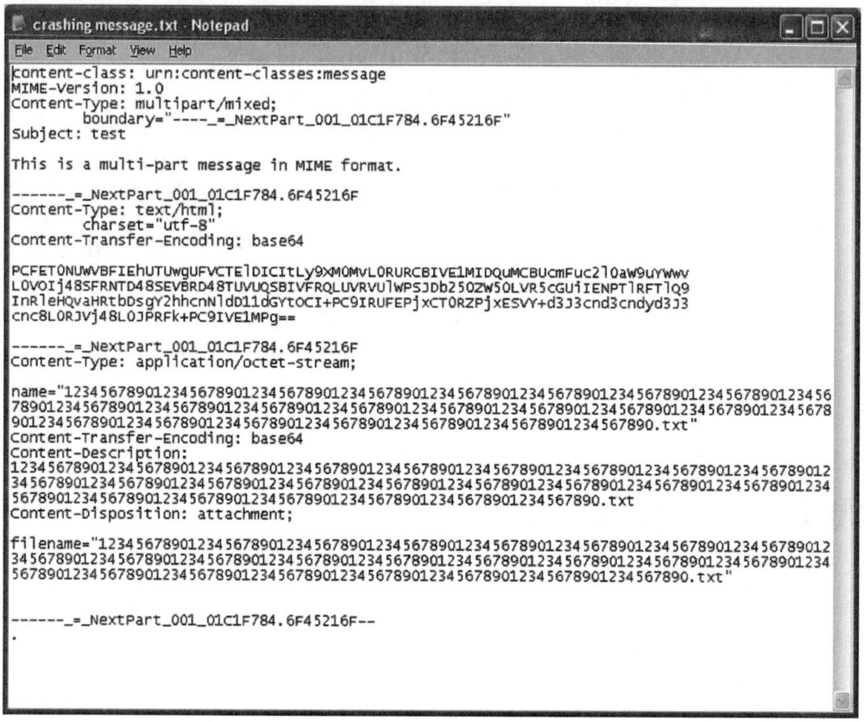

```
crashing message.txt - Notepad
File  Edit  Format  View  Help
content-class: urn:content-classes:message
MIME-Version: 1.0
Content-Type: multipart/mixed;
        boundary="----_=_NextPart_001_01C1F784.6F45216F"
Subject: test

This is a multi-part message in MIME format.

------_=_NextPart_001_01C1F784.6F45216F
Content-Type: text/html;
        charset="utf-8"
Content-Transfer-Encoding: base64

PCFETONUWVBFIEhUTUwgUFVCTElDICItLy9XMQMvLORURCBIVE1MIDQuMCBUcmFuc2l0aW9uYWwv
LOVOIj48SFRNTD48SEVBRD48TUVUQSBIVFRRQLUVRVU1WPSJDb25OZW5OLVR5cGUiIENPQTlRFTlQ9
InRleHQvaHRtbDsgY2hhcnNldD0i1dGYtOCI+PC9IRUFEPjxCT0RZPjxESVY+d3J3cndd3cndyd3J3
cnc8LORJVj48LOJPRFk+PC9IVE1MPg==

------_=_NextPart_001_01C1F784.6F45216F
Content-Type: application/octet-stream;

name="12345678901234567890123456789012345678901234567890123456789012345678901234567890123456
78901234567890123456789012345678901234567890123456789012345678901234567890123456789012345678
90123456789012345678901234567890123456789012345678901234567890.txt"
Content-Transfer-Encoding: base64
Content-Description:
123456789012345678901234567890123456789012345678901234567890123456789012345678901234567890123456789012
34567890123456789012345678901234567890123456789012345678901234567890123456789012345678901234567890123456789012345678901234
56789012345678901234567890123456789012345678901234567890123456789012345678901234567890.txt
Content-Disposition: attachment;

filename="123456789012345678901234567890123456789012345678901234567890123456789012345678901234567890123456789012
34567890123456789012345678901234567890123456789012345678901234567890123456789012345678901234567890123456789012345678901234
56789012345678901234567890123456789012345678901234567890123456789012345678901234567890.txt"


------_=_NextPart_001_01C1F784.6F45216F--
.
```

Figure 2.11 shows our altered test message. By telneting[7] into an open SMTP (Simple Mail Transfer Protocol) port, we can send this message to our test account that Eudora will read from. When we then try to download the message with Eudora, it causes a crash, as shown in Fig. 2.12. To reassure us that the application has indeed crashed, a second error message appears after clicking the "Don't Send" button on the first, as shown in Fig. 2.13. Eudora will continue to crash every time we try to download mail from this account. The only way to get to our mail through Eudora is to connect to the server through another email client and delete the corrupted message.

Crashes like this that involve long strings require special investigation because of their potential to be an exploitable buffer overflow.

---

[7]Telnet is a protocol used to connect in a terminal fashion to certain network ports to exchange raw data in text form.

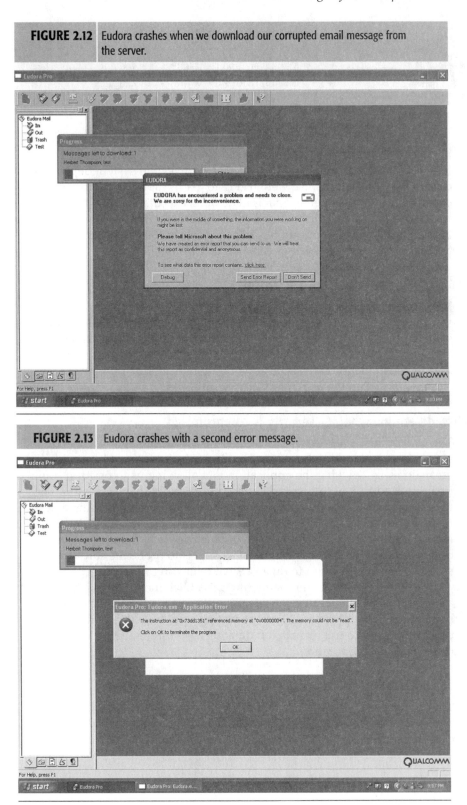

FIGURE 2.12 Eudora crashes when we download our corrupted email message from the server.

FIGURE 2.13 Eudora crashes with a second error message.

ATTACK 4   Manipulate and replace files that the application creates, reads from, writes to, or executes

WHEN to apply this attack

Like the last attack, this fourth attack also involves file-system dependencies. In previous attacks, we were trying to get the application to process corrupt data. In this one, we manipulate data, executables, or libraries in ways that force the application to behave insecurely. This attack can be applied any time an application reads or writes to the file system, launches another executable, or accesses functionality from a library.

WHAT faults make this attack successful?

Like the registry, applications tend to trust the file system as an input source. In the case of libraries and executables, this trust is almost universally implicit. The wild card here, though, is that if these files can be altered by a user (authorized or unauthorized) to gain access to sensitive data or functionality, then security will be compromised, no matter how closely input from the user interface is scrutinized.

HOW to determine whether security is compromised

The goal of this attack is to test whether the application allows us to do something we shouldn't be able to do. Of particular interest is privilege escalation—i.e., tricking the application into allowing us to perform some unauthorized task or to access data that we shouldn't have access to. The tell-tale sign that something has gone wrong in this case is gaining access to another user's data or functionality. When the application reads our altered file and there is no overt sign of an error, such as an error message or an application hang or crash, the next step is to probe the software and see what it will allow you to do and what data you can read.

A common result while conducting this attack though is for the application to crash because we altered a file and inadvertently passed bad data to the application. More interesting results occur when the application tries to use this altered data for user authentication or some other internal computation.

HOW to conduct this attack

The approach here is similar to that of the previous attack: First we watch the application and see which files it accesses. Next we try to determine when each file is accessed and for what purpose. In Windows, using Holodeck, this can be done by watching the application's file operations as the software executes and looking for suspicious file accesses. We are looking for data files as well as libraries that can be replaced with malicious or Trojaned versions. This attack can really be an eye opener. Not many testers—or developers, for that matter—have a big-picture perspective on when their application is writing out data to or reading data from the file system.

One class of software that is particularly at risk are Web applications that use cookies. From a privacy and security perspective, cookies are one of the most controversial mechanisms of data storage. They use plain text to store information on a client's machine to preserve "state" for a Web application. Usually they are used to keep track of navigation history through a Website or to store user information to automatically recognize users when they return to a particular Web page. In some instances, the data stored is even more elaborate. Many e-commerce applications use them to keep track of the items in a user's "shopping cart" while they browse other items on that site.

Cookies can be dangerous, because often they are the single means of verifying facts about Website users. Some of the most trivial examples of this are Websites that offer users a trial period in which to use their services before they have to either "register" (which usually means giving personal information that can be used for marketing purposes), pay for the service, or both. In these cases, just deleting the relevant cookies from your machine can get around these checks. Of more concern, though, is when log-in information, such as a unique user-identification number, is stored in a cookie. Sometimes just manually changing this value with a text editor can give one user access to another user's account.

ATTACK 5   Force the application to operate in low memory, disk-space, and network-availability conditions

WHEN to apply this attack

An application is a set of instructions for computer hardware to execute. First, the computer will load the application into memory and then give the application additional memory in which to store and manipulate its internal data. Memory is only temporary, though; to really be useful, an application needs to store persistent data. That's where the file system comes in, and with it, the need for disk space. Without sufficient memory or disk space, most applications will not be able to perform their intended function.

A third physical resource that many modern applications rely on is the network. Many applications rely on shared data or resources available through a network share. Thus testing failure scenarios is a pre-release priority.

Depriving the application of any of these resources allows testers to understand how robust their application is under stress. The decision regarding which failure scenarios to try (and when) can only be determined on a case-by-case basis. A general rule of thumb is to block a resource when an application seems most in need of it. For memory, this may be during some intense computation the application is performing. For disk errors, look for intense periods of file writes and reads by the application; it is in these situations that the application is vulnerable to disk errors.

For the network, one of the greatest benefits of this attack is gaining an understanding of your application's dependence on remote resources. From a security point of view, this understanding is critical, because the network represents a system's most direct route to the outside world. Complete network failure can be produced by simply unplugging the network cable, but this isn't the only type of network fault that can occur in practice. With Holodeck we can simulate this and other more obscure errors without having to disconnect or destroy hardware and cables.

WHAT faults make this attack successful?

As with the other attacks in this chapter, unhandled (or poorly handled) failures can leave the application vulnerable. Specifically, for memory, disk space and the network, developers rarely run into these situations during production. They usually have powerful machines and a network environment that is ideally suited to running their application. They are in the business of software, so it is likely that their network is more reliable than those of some of their software's users. It's not surprising that many resource failures that occur in practice aren't encountered by developers. For this reason, software tends to be very vulnerable in these stressed situations.

HOW to determine whether security is compromised

There are a few specific signs to look for:

- **Memory:** When conventional memory is low, software turns to the hard disk to store its data using some form of a swap file. If hackers can read the swap file, they can often uncover internal information about the application. For example, if the software requires a registration number or "CD key" to fully install, hackers can study the swap file at various stages of the installation process and figure out how to bypass these mechanisms. Some software tries to prevent these types of attacks by preventing debuggers from attaching during runtime, so that memory cannot be read directly. However, if we force the software to use a swap file, the data is available without a debugger.

- **Disk Space:** When the OS denies requests for disk space, applications often find themselves in uncharted territory. CreateFile and other system calls start to fail in obscure places in the code. If error handlers are not in place, the application will fail. Such failures usually take the form of an application crash. It is important to investigate these situations in the test lab, especially for mission-critical applications.

- **Network:** Many modern applications are so integrated with remote resources that a failed network can cripple them. Although network connections may be critical to the application functioning properly, it is important to investigate the impact of network failure on security. Of most concern are failures that prevent the application from performing some critical security-related task that requires access to a remote machine—for example, remote authentication and logging. Another common failure is that the application may write out sensitive data to a file temporarily while it is waiting for the network to become available.

HOW to conduct this attack

Creating competition among different programs for the file system and memory can be accomplished directly by launching lots of applications and creating large files on disk. Another quick and dirty option is to create a simple application with an infinite loop that writes to a file until the hard drive is full or allocates memory until the machine has no more to give. Similarly, the network can be strained by starting a few sizable downloads.

For Windows applications, life is much simpler. We can simulate these failures at runtime using Holodeck. Fig. 2.14 shows Holodeck's

FIGURE 2.14 Holodeck can insert a wide variety of network, disk, and memory failures into the application.

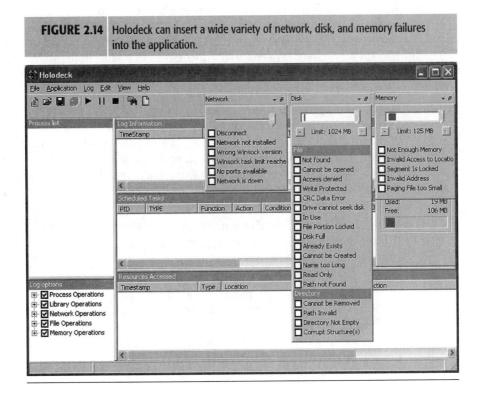

menus for specific network, disk, and memory faults it can inject into a running application.

Use a performance monitoring tool such as TaskManager (which ships with Windows) or Microsoft's PerfMon to search for points at which memory, disk, or network usage increases while running a particular application. Next, use Holodeck to selectively deny these resources to the application. Many times an application will hang or crash, especially when memory or disk space is deprived. Many of these crashes will be uninteresting from a security perspective, so look for actions that are not being performed because of the lack of a resource, such as writing log-on attempts to a remote log. If this is the case, when the network cable is unplugged, the attacker can execute unlimited log-in attempts on the local machine with impunity. Also look for other actions that are being performed because of missing resources, such as writing sensitive information out to a swap file as a result of a lack of memory.

Summary of the Dependency Attacks: A Checklist for Battle

1. List the libraries that your application uses. For each one, try to (1) figure out what service it provides to the application and when the application loads this library for use, and (2) selectively deny the application access to these libraries and watch for failures.

2. Find out which registry values your application reads and writes. The best way to isolate interesting registry keys is to watch the application during installation and startup under Holodeck. After you've identified the keys, look for sensitive information stored in the registry and tamper with keys that may be read at startup to try to get the program to expose data or functionality.

3. Watch your application run under Holodeck and look at documentation to uncover the files and file types your application reads. Next, start corrupting these files with long strings, escape characters, and commands, and observe how the application responds. The potential payoff is a "safe" file (like a music file) that a user downloads and trusts that can exploit a vulnerability in the application to execute commands (through script, buffer overflows, etc.).

4. Using the files and libraries you identified in the previous attacks, try to alter them in such a way as to make the application behave insecurely. Good targets are files used to store configuration information or application data (such as cookies).

5. Launch your application under Holodeck and observe whether your software can securely handle disk, memory, and network errors. The application may crash or hang, but watch for subtle symptoms of security breaches, such as sensitive data being written to the hard drive or dumped to the screen or a file.

Conclusion

Software depends on a variety of external resources that are crucial to getting its work done. As testers, it is our responsibility to ensure that external component failures do not compromise the integrity of the application and its data. The five attacks this chapter has discussed provide a good starting point for testing that the application responds securely to dependency failures. Running through the attacks will help you weed out some of these vulnerabilities; as a side benefit, you will learn a lot about which resources your application needs and when.

Exercises

Identifying an application's dependencies is the first step in assessing how secure that application really is. After all, an application is only as secure as the libraries, files, and other resources the application depends on. Professional testers can use the application they are currently working with to answer the questions that follow. For students, we usually select two or three applications before the semester begins and then work through these exercises on each. The advantage of choosing several targets is that some applications have classes of dependencies that others don't. Pick your target application or feature and answer the following questions:

1. Use Holodeck (if you're testing on Windows) or some other library tool to find out which libraries your application loads. For professional testers, look at internal documentation and talk to developers to gain information about the libraries you find. For students, search the Internet for documentation and find out:

    a. Who provides the library? Is it a part of the operating system, the application, or from a third party?

    b. From what you have uncovered in part (a), describe in one paragraph the services that each library provides to your application.

    c. When are the libraries loaded? Is it when some particular action is performed?

2. If your application runs on the Windows operating system, identify which registry keys that your application creates to store data. Holodeck will allow you to observe registry writes and identify these keys. Sometimes the amount of interaction between an application and the registry can be voluminous. Watch your application install, and identify which new registry keys it creates. For each key or group of keys, look at the name of the key and the data it holds, and write down in one sentence which data you think the application stores there, and what the application uses that data for.

3. Identify all of the files and file types that your application reads, writes to, or uses. One way to compile this list is to watch the application run under Holodeck.

   a. For each file, determine which category(s) it falls into:

      i. Library or a file containing executable commands (dll, file containing script, etc.).

      ii. File used by the application to store data (database, text file, log, etc.).

      iii. Read-only file (one that can be viewed but not edited).

   b. For each file, identify whether it is a local resource (read from the same machine that the application is running on) or a remote resource (read from a server on the Internet or intranet).

4. For this exercise, we will be using Holodeck's fault-injection features. Run your target application under Holodeck.

   a. Identify the memory-intensive operations that your application performs. Pay particular attention to security-related operations such as encryption.

   b. For the features you identified in part (a), try the memory faults in Holodeck and observe the results. Does the application crash? Is data dumped to a file or to the screen?

5. Use your answers from the previous questions to apply each of the dependency attacks to your application. Document the tests you tried, the features that behaved securely in the presence of the hostile environment you created, blatant security bugs, and suspicious behavior.

CHAPTER 3
Breaking Security Through the User Interface

011001011101100011001100

The user interface is usually the most comfortable bug hunting ground for testers. It's the way we are accustomed to interacting with our applications, and the way application developers expect us to. The attacks discussed in this chapter focus on inputs applied to software through its user interface.

The fault model in Chapter 1 tells us that most security bugs result from additional, unintended, and undocumented user behavior. From the UI (User Interface), this amounts to handling unexpected input from the user in a way that compromises the application, the system it runs on, or its data. The result could be privilege escalation (a normal user acquiring administrative rights) or allowing secret information to be viewed by an unauthorized user.

Ideally, the attacks presented in this chapter should be conducted one at a time, so that you can focus on a specific class of vulnerability. Don't get too carried away on any one attack, though. For example, when looking for buffer overflows, just concentrate on feeding long strings to input fields; other attacks are more effective at looking for bugs that have to do with other types of malicious input.

| ATTACK **6** | Overflow input buffers |

WHEN to apply this attack

Buffer overflows are by far the most notorious security problems in software. They occur when applications fail to properly constrain input length. Some buffer overflows don't present much of a security threat. Others, however, can allow hackers to take control of a system by sending a well-crafted string to the application. This second type is referred to by the industry as "exploitable," because parts of the string may get executed if they are interpreted as code. What sometimes happens is that a fixed amount of memory is allocated to hold user input. If developers then fail to constrain the length of the input strings entered by the user, data can over-write application instructions, allowing the user to execute arbitrary code.

Most high-level programming languages are essentially immune to buffer overflows, either because they detect and prevent them explicitly (Ada95) or because they automatically resize arrays (Perl). Unfortunately, the most dominant programming languages for commercial application development, C and C++, provide minimal to no protection against such problems. Low-level routines, written in assembly for example, do not pro-tect against buffer overflows, either. This doesn't mean that if your applica-tion is written in a "safe" language, it is immune to buffer-overflow prob-lems; the reason is that many library routines, along with routines that call them, are written in C or C++. It is the interactions between the applica-tions and these routines that can still leave open the possibility of a buffer overflow.

This attack is applicable any time software accepts alphanumeric input from a user, whether through the GUI, via the command prompt, or by using APIs.

WHAT faults make this attack successful?

The fault here is that a particular input has an *assumed*, but not *enforced*, length. For example, take a Web application that asks for your ZIP code to be entered into a text field. Developers may assume that such inputs will be, at most, nine digits and a hyphen. This data may then be extracted and sent to a back-end server application without any checks performed by the client. Now imagine a malicious user pasting a 200-page document into this field. If the server application doesn't perform checks on the data handed off to it, the results can be unpredictable. In the worst case, a string can contain executable content that the server runs, which means that a user entering data into a browser form can cause code to be executed on a remote server.

HOW to determine whether security is compromised

When application commands get overwritten by random input, the appli-cation will typically crash. This makes detection pretty easy most of the time; simply send long strings and wait for the software to fail. A buffer overflow that causes the application to crash is usually enough to convince wise managers that you've found a problem that needs to be fixed. The forensics necessary to determine whether the buffer overflow is exploitable can be time consuming. This class of fault, though, usually inspires enough fear (rightly so) to motivate a fix *without* such forensics.

HOW to conduct this attack

The first step is to identify an interesting input field as a target. From a security perspective, look for data that is gathered from an untrusted user through a Web interface or even data files. Another rich source of these types of bugs are applications that run at a higher privilege level than their users are authorized for. Successful attacks here would allow a user to execute commands at the enhanced privilege level of the running application. An example would be the infamous buffer overflow in sendmail.

Code Red: An Overflow of $2 Billion

On July 18, 2002, the Code Red II worm was unleashed on the Internet and analysts estimate that more than 359,000 machines were infected within fourteen hours. The worm continued to spread and caused more than an estimated $2 billion in damage worldwide. The Code Red virus was not written to cause major damage to the host; rather, it devoured network bandwidth by searching out other vulnerable hosts on the network to infect. The worm exploits a buffer-overflow vulnerability in Microsoft's Internet Information Server (IIS), which allows a remote user to execute arbitrary instructions remotely on an unpatched web server.

After you have identified a target, a good technique is to start with the string 123456789[1]. You can test the limits of that field by pasting this string and increasing the length by 10 each time. Explore the limits of the field and look for points at which you are physically constrained from adding any more characters. If you reach this point, and the application correctly processes your input, then developers have done their job, and there is no buffer-overflow concern.

If the application doesn't physically constrain input length, the next step is to look for error messages. Error messages that quote the offending string are a sign that the application is storing that string somewhere, and there is a good chance of a crash with longer strings. If you don't receive any error messages and the input length is unconstrained, there are three possibilities:

1. The input length still is not long enough to raise an error message or to cause the application to misbehave. If this happens, continue to increase string size in additional test cases.

---

[1]Included on the CD-ROM is a Word document (longstrings.doc), which contains a series of long strings that can be easily copied and pasted into your application's input fields.

2. A long string processed from this field does not cause the application to fail.

3. Data is truncated internally by the application, and there is no buffer-overflow concern.

There are many buffer-overflow examples on bugtraq (available at www.securityfocus.com), CERT (www.cert.org) and other Websites. One of the most widely publicized buffer overflows was one in Microsoft's Internet Information Server (IIS), which was exploited by the Code Red and Nimda viruses (see sidebar). This bug ended up causing billions of dollars in damage as a result of lost revenue world wide. Don't let this happen to your software!

ATTACK 7   Examine all common switches and options

WHEN to apply this attack

Some applications are tolerant to varying user input under a default configuration. Most default configurations are chosen by the application developers, and most tests are executed under these conditions, especially if options are obscure or are entered using command-line switches. When these configurations are changed, the software is often forced to use code paths that may be severely under-tested and thus results can be unpredictable.

Obviously, to test a wide range of inputs under every possible set of configurations is impossible for large applications; instead, this attack focuses on some of the more obscure configurations. The most revealing situations we've come across are those in which switches are set through the command line at startup.

The best-case scenario would be to execute a core set of tests under every conceivable configuration; the problem is that the number of possible combinations can be staggering. Consider, for example, the Advanced tab of the Internet Options dialog box on Microsoft's Internet Explorer (see Fig. 3.1). Ideally, we would like to run a series of tests under each possible combination of options. However, this tab contains fifty-two check boxes, each of which can be selected or not, resulting in 2^{52} possible configurations—over four thousand trillion different execution environments! Obviously, it is impossible to execute meaningful tests in all of these environments. In practice, many options are not likely to impact the outcome of certain tests, and, similarly, several options are likely to be unrelated to each other. A more manageable scenario is to consider options in groups of two or three. Some commercial tools, such as Telecordia's AETG Web Service, can be configured to determine the optimal environments and test cases through the selection of options to meet testing objectives.

FIGURE 3.1	The Advanced tab of Internet Explorer's Internet Options dialog box contains fifty-two checkboxes, resulting in over four thousand trillion possible combinations!

WHAT faults make this attack successful?

The problem here is that developers may not consider all of the possible configurations of the software as they attempt to secure input. This means that some code paths will include security procedures, whereas others may be left unguarded. This is particularly common when the infamous "penetrate and patch" method—finding a security bug and implementing a fix for it—is used rather than implementing security in the design from the beginning. Bugs uncovered under common operating configurations might be patched, but the bigger problem of securing the same behavior under other possible configurations still remains.

HOW to determine whether security is compromised

Most of the vulnerabilities we've found using this attack appeared in the command line using switches. In these cases, a particular switch forces the application to execute under-exercised code. The result, for the most part, has been getting around input filters for strings sent to the application through the command line. Improperly constrained strings can translate into buffer-overflow vulnerabilities and improper handling of escape characters, character sets, and commands. This is why this particular attack ties in so well with the other two in this chapter. Failures in this area are likely to take the same form as those addressed in the other two attacks—namely, an application crash because of code with a long parameter value or using special characters as parameter values.

HOW to conduct this attack

For multiversion software[2], go back to previous releases and documentation and look for obscure switches and options that may have been used but are conspicuously missing from the current specification or help documentation.

Most of the time when developers embark on a new version of an application, the existing code base is enhanced with additional features, and some code (like "if" statements when some command line switch is used) may be left unaltered. When you find these switches, test input parameters with long strings and escape characters using the techniques in Attacks 6 and 8.

Another good strategy is to pick configurations and options that are likely to be underrepresented during functional testing or are likely to execute legacy functionality. Remember that security measures are more likely to be implemented correctly on code paths that are most frequently executed and on scenarios that are most obvious to developers and test managers. For command-line arguments and options that influence the size or type of data permitted in a certain field or parameter, serious problems occur when the input changes and validation routines remain the same. Some of the best examples are Web applications that ask for user credit-card information.

Imagine a field marked "postal code" and a drop-down menu containing a list of countries for the user to select from, as shown in Fig. 3.2. There may be logic built into the web page (through client-side scripts) or server validation of the input that constrains the postal code field to ten characters (a five digit zip, a dash, and a four digit suffix) once the country selected is the United States. U.S. developers may be unfamiliar with the length and composition of foreign postal codes and thus may not write validation routines for that data; this is where the application becomes vulnerable. When the country value changes, the user may then be given free reign to enter a string of any length and containing any character. This can lead to

---

[2]Many applications go through multiple releases. A good example is Microsoft's Word word-processing application, which we used to write this book. Word is on its tenth public release, in addition to the numerous updates and patches that were released to create small incremental versions. For security testing purposes, we can consider each new build or patched application as a new version. It is our job as testers to ensure that bugs don't slip in between versions.

serious vulnerabilities if the data is processed by functions that have allocated a limited amount of space for the value or are susceptible to escape
characters altering control flow. Enabling these types of options creates a
good opportunity to try Attacks 6 and 8 on the now-exposed input fields.

FIGURE 3.2	Data contained in the "ZIP/Postal Code" field may be constrained well by the client or server when the United States is the selected country. However, developers may not do such a good job with some other countries, for which postal-code data may not go through validation routines.

Checkout - Microsoft Internet Explorer

File Edit View Favorites Tools Help

Back · | Search Favorites Media

Address C:\Documents and Settings\Herbert Thompson\My Documents\misc\examplepage.htm

Enter the shipping address for this order.
Enter the name and address where you'd like us to ship your order. Please also indicate whether your billing address is the same
as the shipping address entered. When you're done, click the Continue button.

Full Name:	Herbert Thompson
Address Line 1	
Address Line 2	
City:	
State/Province/Region:	
ZIP/Postal Code:	01234567890123456789
Country:	Christmas Island
Phone Number:	

Is this address also your billing address? ● Yes
○ No (If not, we'll ask you for it in a moment.)

Continue

Done   My Computer

ATTACK 8   Explore escape characters, character sets, and commands

WHEN to apply this attack

Some applications may treat certain characters as equivalent when they
are part of a string. For most purposes, a string with the letter *a* in a certain
position is not likely to be processed any differently from a similar string
with the letter *z* in that same position. With this in mind, the question,
"Which characters or combinations of characters *are* treated differently?"

naturally follows. This is the driving question behind this attack. By forcing the application to process special characters and commands, we can sometimes force it to behave in ways its designers did not intend. Factors that affect which characters and commands might be interpreted differently include the language the application was written in, the

Buffer Overflow Versus Escape-Character Attacks

On the surface, this attack seems very similar to the buffer-overflow attack discussed earlier; indeed, they both exploit the same flaw of unconstrained input. The difference is that with buffer-overflow attacks, we attempt to send the application a string that is too long for the memory allocated for it. With some careful appending of low-level commands to the end of this string, the operating system can be deceived into executing these commands rather than, or in addition to, application instructions. To exploit a buffer overflow for the first time usually requires a fairly savvy attacker, because appended commands must be in machine language. Unfortunately, though, attack strings sometimes become widely distributed and then the so-called "**script kiddie**" (see Glossary) class of attacker can exploit these weaknesses, too.

Escape character attacks use special characters embedded in strings of usually normal length to force the application to execute commands. Since many of these escape sequences are standard, a minimally skilled hacker can potentially craft a string which executes unauthorized commands. This means that the knowledge necessary to exploit an escape character vulnerability for the first time is minimal, which makes these types of bugs as, or more, dangerous than buffer overflows.

SQL Injection

The Structured Query Language (SQL) is an ANSI standard language for accessing data from a relational database. SQL is commonly used to process user-supplied data from Web pages and applications on the server side. *SQL Injection* is a technique for inserting SQL commands as user input. If these inputs are not properly filtered for escape characters and commands, an attacker can potentially append data and commands to an SQL query, which may force the server to send back sensitive information, overwrite other user's data on the server, or execute server commands.

The problem stems from the fact that SQL commands on a Web server are typically constructed based on data received from users. As an example, consider a log-in mechanism in which usernames and passwords are stored in a database and a query is constructed based on authentication information supplied by a user on a Web form. An example of such a string constructed on an Active Server Page (ASP) may be

(continued)
```
QueryName = "SELECT Username FROM
AuthenticationTable WHERE Username = '" &
Request.Form("Name") & "'Password = '" &
Request.Form("Password") & "'"
```

In the query above, if a valid username/password combination is entered, the name of that authenticated user is stored in the variable QueryName. One simple check to see whether the username/password combination is valid is to check to see whether this variable contains any data. If it contains a nonempty string, the user is granted access and that user's credentials are forwarded on. One easy way to subvert such a mechanism is to change the query to

```
  SELECT Username FROM AuthenticationTable
WHERE TRUE
```

which will result in the first username in the table being stored in the variable QueryName. This can be accomplished by entering

```
  Username: ' OR '1'='1
  Password: ' OR '1'='1
```

This will force everything after the WHERE clause to equate to TRUE and return the first name in the table to the variable QueryName.

There are many other tricks you can try with SQL injection. For example, many SQL commands are passed from page to page or to the server using GET. GET exposes data in the browser's URL, which is then easily modified by an attacker. If you are testing any Web-based application or an application that sends commands to a database, you need to try SQL injection attacks, or hackers will do it for you.

libraries that user data is passed through, and specific words and strings reserved by the underlying operating system.

WHAT faults make this attack successful?

Like buffer overflows, the faults exploitable with this attack result from poorly constrained input. Consider a simple Web page. Most web applications gather user information through forms. The traditional validation approach for data entered into a form relies on client-side scripts, such as JavaScript code, to ensure that important fields are not left blank and that numeric data is within a certain range. Once these cursory checks are performed, however, there is usually an implicit trust of this data. Malicious users can exploit this trust and enter data that may get executed on the remote server.

Form data is especially suspect, because it is easy to manipulate and typically gets processed by some application that interprets values as more than just text. One particularly dangerous instance is when form data is dumped onto a subsequent Web page. For example, to create a rapport with the user, a Web application may require you to enter a first name into a form field with the tag UserName. On a subsequent page, the user's name may be included in a welcome message such as

```
<b>Welcome <%=Request.Form("UserName")%>,</b>
```

If, however, :

```
<SCRIPT LANGUAGE="JavaScript">Form1.Hidden1.value =
"bigtrouble"; </SCRIPT>,
```

was entered as a username, hard-coded hidden tags within the HTML (Hyper Text Markup Language) document could be easily modified.[3] Suppose that the user had a Submit option on this page; if so, subsequent pages would probably implicitly trust the value associated with this hidden tag. To prevent these issues, raw data should be processed by HTML encoding it with a function such as VBScript's Server.HTMLencode. The above welcome message would now read

```
<b>Welcome
<%=Server.HTMLEncode(Request.Form("UserName"))%>,</b>
```

When form data is processed by the server, other risks must also be considered. If the form is parsed by a CGI (Common Gateway Interface) script escape sequences can be used to execute malicious commands on the server. No data sent from a previous page should be trusted. Risks must be assessed and appropriate server validation should be used to augment client-side error checks.

Data passed from page to page using the GET[4] method is exposed and modifiable by the user simply by changing values in the URL. Such data should be considered completely under the control of the user. In this case, client-side input-constraint mechanisms (such as validating input using JavaScript before you can hit the Submit button) become useless, because the user can still modify the raw data before it gets processed.

---

[3]Certainly there are other ways of modifying hidden tags such as manipulating the POST stream; saving the page, altering the HTML and reposting the form; among others.

[4]The two most common methods of transferring data between web pages are the GET and POST methods. With GET, data is passed as parameters in the URL. This data is thus easily readable and changeable by even the most technologically challenged Web user. Using POST, data is passed in the HTTP header and is thus not directly visible or changeable by the user. This data is still under the control of the tech-savvy user, however, and can be passed by creating a separate Web page and then posting altered data to the original target page.

The source of POST data can also be suspect. If a malicious user creates a page that posts data to a waiting page on a remote server, they have complete control of data sent, including data in hidden tags, which is rarely validated. Such situations can be avoided by verifying the referring page. This information can be extracted from the server variable HTTP_REFERER, which should always be checked (but unfortunately this information can also be faked).

HOW to determine whether security is compromised

There are two major concerns to consider. The first is a possible denial-of-service attack by sending bad input to a remote application that causes either the application or the entire system to crash or hang. The second concern is that an input string can be crafted to force the application to perform unauthorized actions. This is highly dependent on the mechanism used to process user-input data. Web-based applications are probably the most susceptible to this type of attack.

Typically, an Internet application has at least two distinct parts: a form that *gathers* user data and a server application that *processes* the user data. Each component may rely on the other to filter user input. If neither does its job, data may be passed as arguments into functions that can interpret certain strings as commands.

HOW to conduct this attack

First, get to know your application by getting answers to such questions as

1. What operating system does your application run on?
2. What language(s) is it written in?
3. What libraries, scripts, databases, and external applications does user data get passed to?
4. What are the character sets, reserved words, commands, and so on, that your application's components use?

Answering these questions is a good place to start planning your attack. You can also use Table 3.1 to help craft your attack strings.

TABLE 3.1 Escape and Special Characters for Various Platforms and Applications

Character Values	ASCII Values	Applicability	Use	Fault Model
NUL (^@)	0	O/S; Windows	MS-DOS uses NUL-terminated strings in system functions	Embedded nulls may affect strings used for system calls. NUL may cause all characters following it to be ignored.

TABLE 3.1		Escape and Special Characters for Various Platforms and Applications *(Cont.)*		
Character Values	**ASCII Values**	**Applicability**	**Use**	**Fault Model**
		O/S; UNIX	UNIX uses NUL-terminated strings for all system functions.	Embedded nulls may affect strings used for system calls. NUL may cause all characters following it to be ignored.
		Language; C, C++ and others	C and C++ use NUL as the string termination character for all standard library functions	Embedded nulls may affect any string input field. NUL may cause all characters following it to be ignored.
ETX (^C)	3	Shell; Windows	MS-DOS uses ETX as the program-interrupt character.	Program may interrupt upon input of ETX.
		Shell; UNIX	UNIX shells use ETX as the program interrupt character	Program may interrupt upon input of ETX.
EOT (^D)	4	O/S; UNIX	UNIX uses EOT as the text end-of-file character.	EOT may have a wide range of effects in input strings; characters after input may be ignored; input or program may terminate, or unpredictable behavior might occur.
		Shell; UNIX	Many UNIX shells use EOT as the end-of-transmission character.	EOT may cause the application or shell to terminate.
SOH, ENQ, ACK, VT, SO, SI, DLE, DC2, DC4, NAK, SYN, ETB, EM, FS, GS, RS, US	Various	All	Miscellaneous non-printing characters.	Legacy characters from teletypes with no fixed modern use. May be used as sentinel values in strings. May cause emission of non-ASCII character.
BEL (^G)	7	All	Audible bell character.	May cause the audible bell to be rung during input or output of the string; may leave an embedded bell character in persistent data.

TABLE 3.1 Escape and Special Characters for Various Platforms and Applications *(Cont.)*

Character Values	ASCII Values	Applicability	Use	Fault Model
BS (^H)	8	O/S; Windows	Backspace	May cause backspace to be embedded in persistent data. May cause backspacing or cursor movement without visible effect.
		Shell; UNIX	Backspace	Some shells and applications use BS as the backspace character, whereas others use DEL. May cause persistent data and display problems.
TAB (^I)	9	All	Horizontal Tab	Tab key may be expanded as spaces unintentionally in persistent data, or may remain a TAB character when it should be expanded.
LF (^J)	10	O/S; Windows	Linefeed	Windows uses CR/LF as a linespace character. Extra LFs may cause persistent data problems.
		O/S; UNIX	Linefeed	LF is used as a linespace character. May embed linespaces unintentionally.
		Compatibility	Linefeed	UNIX uses LF as the linespace, whereas Windows uses CR/LF. Many possible problems.
FF (^L)	12	Shell; UNIX	Formfeed	May cause scrolling or other problems in some shells.
		All	Formfeed	May cause display and especially printing problems with persistent data if embedded.
CR (^M)	13	All	*See LF*	
		All	Carriage Return	May cause functions assigned CTRL-M to be unachievable.
DC1, DC3 (^Q, ^S)	17, 19	Shell; UNIX	XON/XOFF	Terminal handshaking characters. DC3 may cause input echo to freeze, looking like a lock-up. DC1 may not perform its assigned function, transmitting the XON signal instead.

TABLE 3.1   Escape and Special Characters for Various Platforms and Applications *(Cont.)*

Character Values	ASCII Values	Applicability	Use	Fault Model
CAN (^X)	24	Shell; Windows	Causes previous text to be canceled and new input to be taken.	May cause previous inputs to be ignored.
		Shell; UNIX	Causes previous text to be canceled.	May cause previous inputs to be ignored.
SUB (^Z)	26	O/S; Windows	Text end-of-file character.	SUB may have a wide range of effects in input strings; characters after input may be ignored; input or program may terminate, or unpredictable behavior might occur.
		Shell; UNIX	Shell escape character. SUB is used to suspend the running program and escape to the shell.	May cause program execution to be suspended.
SPACE	32	Shell; UNIX	Space is used to delimit arguments in some programs.	Embedded spaces may have undesirable effects if the string is to be later treated as an argument.
!	33	Shell; UNIX	Used to expand a history command in some shells.	The ! may be expanded when used as part of a shell command.
"	34	Language; C, C++, VB, and others	Quotations are used to delimit strings in many languages.	Mismatched quotes, embedded quotes, etc., may cause undesirable behavior if the strings are later interpreted or processed.
# ( ) , - . / @ [ ] : ; = ^ _ { } ~	Various		No known side effects.	
$	36	Shell; UNIX	The $ is used as the environment character.	May expand the token with its environment variable value; e.g., $1.00 might expand to <value of argument-1>.0.

TABLE 3.1   Escape and Special Characters for Various Platforms and Applications *(Cont.)*

Character Values	ASCII Values	Applicability	Use	Fault Model
%	37	Shell; Windows	The % is used as the environment-expansion character.	May expand the token with its environment variable value; e.g,. 10%20% might expand to 10<value of variable "20">.
		Language; C, C++	The % character is used as the argument expansion character in certain string functions.	May cause crashes, data corruption, and other problems if % is interpreted to mean a function-argument expansion in a string.
&	38	Shell; UNIX	Suspend character. Causes shell invocation to run in background.	May cause background running of shell commands with accompanying timing and security problems.
'	39	Language; Pascal, Fortran, Ada and others	*See ".*	
*	42	Shell; Windows and UNIX	Wildcard character.	May expand in unpredictable ways if interpreted.
+	43	Shell; UNIX	Regular expression character.	May expand in unpredictable ways if interpreted.
<, >,|	60, 62, 124	Shell; UNIX, and Windows	Redirection characters; in certain shells, input can be directed to and from files.	May produce unpredictable results and cause security problems.
?	63	Shell; UNIX	Regular expression character.	May expand in unpredictable ways if interpreted.
0 - 9	48-57		Numbers	
A - Z	6590		Uppercase letters.	

TABLE 3.1 Escape and Special Characters for Various Platforms and Applications *(Cont.)*				
Character Values	**ASCII Values**	**Applicability**	**Use**	**Fault Model**
\	92	Language; C, C++	Escape character. Used to embed nonconforming characters in strings.	May have any number of unusual effects if the string is expanded or interpreted; \000 and \0 produce NUL, \n the newline, \a bell, etc.
a -z	97-122		Lowercase letters.	
DEL	127	Shell; UNIX	See BS.	

Some particularly onerous problems can occur when external databases are involved. If your application uses a third-party database to store information, this can be a good place to start. Try escape characters for SQL commands (see Table 3.1) and see if you can access or overwrite data that you should not be able to access.

Summary of the User-Interface Attacks: A Checklist for Battle

1. Try long strings in every user-input field. Look for inputs taken from remote users first, and then look at data received from users that have fewer privileges than the application itself does.

2. Try alternate configurations of your application. Some vulnerabilities exist only when certain options, such as options that support legacy functionality, are selected. It is important to verify that the user is made aware of the security implications of a certain configuration or option and that the descriptions visible through the GUI reflect the true state of the application and system. Also look for new inputs that the application processes under different configurations or inputs that may be processed differently in these situations. After you've identified these inputs, test them with Attacks 6 and 8.

3. Try escape characters, character sets, and commands in input strings. Find out which languages your application and its dependencies are written in. This will help you make better decisions regarding which characters and character sequences to try.

Conclusion

Attacking security vulnerabilities through the user interface is probably the most comfortable place for software testers, and can yield some of the most insidious and dangerous security bugs. These types of faults tend to get noticed and fixed quickly because most of them can be exploited by a hostile user. Although this chapter has the fewest number of attacks, these techniques may prove to find the greatest number of bugs. It's worth spending some time going through each attack in depth. Don't get discouraged if you don't find a buffer overflow or escape character bug after the first ten, twenty, or fifty input fields. These types of bugs may take a while to uncover, but those that you do find are likely to result in some spectacular security failures.

Exercises

The following exercises have been designed to help you to better apply the attacks of this chapter. Professional testers can use whichever application they are currently working with. When we teach these techniques at Florida Tech, we usually pick an application before the semester begins, and then students apply the attacks to this application. Students working on their own will ideally select an application with many inputs, some of which are delivered remotely.

After you've selected your application, perform the following exercises:

1. Pick a feature of your application that has less than fifty string inputs. For each input, determine the maximum length of data that is allowed by pasting in long strings until you are physically limited in size by the application from entering any more data. Try to get the application to process that data and write down the results for each field.

2. For the same feature you selected in Exercise 1, change configuration options, such as check boxes and option buttons, and see whether you can make any other input fields available. If you can, apply the same techniques used in Exercise 1.

3. Work through all of the option and configuration screens of your application. Make a note of the options that are selected by default. Next, find any application documentation that may exist that is packaged with the product. Are there any discrepancies between what the application's stated default behavior is (according to the documentation) and the actual default options you discovered?

4. Pick a feature of your application. List all of the libraries and external applications that process the data received through that feature's

interface. For libraries that are shipped with your application, identify the language in which they were written. Also, for the inputs you identified in Exercises 1 and 2, determine whether any of the strings are treated as more than just text—e.g., whether they contain formatting commands (HTML tags, etc.), are used in computations (numeric values), etc. Based on this information, create three test strings that include escape characters and commands for each of the processed inputs you identified.

5. Use the information you gathered in Exercises 1–4 to apply the attacks in this chapter to your application. Write down what you did, and note any obvious vulnerabilities or suspicious behavior.

References

1. Cooperative Association for Internet Data Analysis, "CAIDA Analysis of Code-Red," http://www.caida.org/analysis/security/code-red/.

PART 3

Design and Implementation Attacks

CHAPTER 4
Attacking Design

It is very difficult to look at 300 pages of design documentation and determine whether the finished product will be secure. It is no surprise then that some security vulnerabilities creep in at the design phase. The problem is that subtle design decisions can lead to component interaction and inherent flaws that create vulnerabilities in the finished product. This chapter will discuss attacks that help expose these design insecurities in software; it will tackle insecure defaults, test accounts, test instrumentation, open ports, and poor constraints on user-supplied program logic.

In this chapter, we will use Holodeck to look for test instrumentation, and a port scanner (included on the accompanying CD-ROM) to find open communication ports. Detailed descriptions of these tools and a discussion of their use are included in the Appendix A.

| ATTACK 9 | Try common default and test account names and passwords |

WHEN to apply this attack

In applications that have restrictions on data and functionality, all users are not treated equally. User actions are governed by their assigned level of access. In most instances, users are identified and authenticated with user names and passwords. Many applications, however, ship with some special user accounts built in; the most common examples being the "Administrator" or "root" accounts. These accounts usually don't present a problem; they are typically well documented, and the user is prompted to change or initialize the password upon installation. Problems arise, though, when undocumented, invisible, or unconfigurable accounts ship with the product.

To apply this attack, we must understand when user credentials are entered and checked. Authentication information can be read by the application in many different ways. The most common is a log-in prompt through a GUI. Sometimes user credentials are also cached by the operating system, and applications read these credentials from the OS through APIs. It is important that authentication through both the GUI and APIs be scrutinized.

This attack is designed to weed out "hidden" accounts so that they can be dealt with before release. It is applicable any time an application employs user authentication to control access to internal functionality or user data.

WHAT faults make this attack successful?

There are three reasons that undocumented accounts remain in shipped products:

- **Test Accounts:** Accounts created for testing purposes sometimes make it into post-release binaries. Many test scripts require authentication in order to access some parts of the application. For this reason, test accounts are sometimes hard-coded into the application to enable immediate testing after a build (e.g., build verification tests). The idea is that test accounts will be removed before the application ships. However, schedules often run long, and accounts are forgotten, or worse, some functionality becomes dependent on them, and they become unintentionally integrated into the functioning application.

- **Legacy Support:** Accounts created to support legacy functionality are sometimes used without proper safeguards. Some maintenance and functional accounts may be grandfathered into an application for backward compatibility. These accounts may be properly documented, constrained, and configurable in previous versions but not in the latest release of the software.

- **Poor Documentation:** An undocumented account is as dangerous as a blank password. If an application or system administrator doesn't know an account exists, and that account isn't readily visible through standard GUI panels, then the application is at fault. It is important to ensure that all accounts are easily detectable by a privileged user such as an administrator.

HOW to determine whether security is compromised

Security is compromised whenever an unauthorized user is allowed access to resources through accounts that are either undocumented or are difficult or impossible to configure. The mere *existence* of unprotected or undocumented accounts is a security breach waiting to happen.

HOW to conduct this attack

Table 4.1 shows some common accounts and passwords that can be used as a starting point for this attack. This table is by no means comprehensive, but it does provide a general overview of the most common test and default accounts that ship with software.

In addition, the hacking community offers a wealth of tools and information to help attackers find these accounts. Just knowing a valid username can be a good starting point for a determined hacker who can then run automated tools to "brute force"[1] passwords.

TABLE 4.1   Common default and test accounts and passwords

Username	Passwords	Systems Affected
Administrator	""; Admin; admin; administrator; Administrator; root	Windows, Unix, and many other platforms and applications
Admin	""; Admin; admin; administrator; Administrator; root	Windows, Unix, and many other platforms and applications
db2admin	db2admin	IBM DB2
Demo	""; demo; demos	Many
Guest	""; Guest	Windows
Guest	guest	AIX
IBM	IBM	AIX
Postmaster	""	Unix; Linux
Powerdown	powerdown	Unix; Linux
Rje	rje	Unix; Linux
Root	""; root	Unix; Linux
sa	""	Microsoft SQL server; others

---

[1]"Brute forcing" is a common term used in the hacking community to refer to the cracking of passwords by trying every possible combination. Obviously, this can take quite some time, even with good automation. Also, the threat of brute-forcing passwords has led to many applications instituting a delay between log-in attempts or account lockouts after a certain number of password attempts. Attackers usually proceed by first trying common words and combinations as passwords, which can significantly reduce the time needed.

TABLE 4.1   Common default and test accounts and passwords *(Cont.)*

Username	Passwords	Systems Affected
setup	setup	Unix; Linux
shutdown	""; shutdown	Unix; Linux
sync	""; sync	Unix; Linux
sys	sys; system; bin	Unix; Linux
sysadm	sysadm; admin	Unix; Linux
sysadmin	sysadmin	Unix; Linux
sysbin	sysbin	Unix; Linux
system_admin	""; system_admin	Unix; Linux
test	""; test; Test	Common to many applications
trouble	trouble	Unix; Linux
umountfs	umountfs	Unix; Linux
umountfsys	umountfsys	Unix; Linux
umountsys	umountsys	Unix; Linux
unix	unix	Unix; Linux
uucp	uucp	Unix; Linux
uucpadm	uucpadm	Unix; Linux
web	""; web	Windows; Unix; Linux
webmaster	""; webmaster	Unix; Linux
www	""; www	Unix; Linux

Another good source of these accounts are automated test scripts and harnesses, especially those that may no longer be in use. The key is to understand which features test scripts are designed to exercise and the authentication needed to access those features. Armed with this information, you then need to do some detective work and sift through the script code to determine which accounts are being used to gain access. If these accounts show up in the release version, then security is at risk.

A good approach is to look for documentation or to ask test developers which features specific tests target. Try to reproduce some of the GUI-based scripted tests manually, and look for stumbling blocks, such as an unavailable option that is still selected by the script. Also look for user-name and password prompts and track down how test scripts get past them. Most of the time it will be by authenticating using a test account. You may also discover some test APIs that bypass these security measures. These test APIs can be dangerous if they make it to the released binary. They are the focus of the next attack.

There are many examples of weak and undocumented accounts shipping with software. Table 4.1 is only a taste; for more, see bugtraq at SecurityFocus (www.securityfocus.com) and other security-vulnerability databases.

ATTACK 10　Use Holodeck to expose unprotected test APIs

WHEN to apply this attack

Complex, large-scale applications are often difficult to test effectively by relying on the APIs intended for normal users alone. Sometimes there are multiple builds in a single week, each of which has to go through a suite of verification tests. To meet this demand, many developers include hooks that are used by custom test harnesses. These hooks—and corresponding test APIs—often bypass normal security checks done by the application for the sake of ease of use and efficiency. Developers add them for testers, intending to remove them before the software is released. The problem is that these test APIs become so integrated into the code and the testing process that when the time comes for the software to be released, managers are reluctant to remove them for fear of "destabilizing" the code, potentially causing a major delay in the ship date. It is thus critical to find these dangerous programmatic interfaces and ensure that, if they were to be accessed in the field by hackers, they could not be used to compromise the application, its host system, or user data.

In this attack, we try to expose test APIs. The attack is most effective during the execution of test suites and scripts. By watching the application with Holodeck while automated test suites are running, we can identify testing dlls that are loaded and used, and then evaluate their impact on application security.

WHAT faults make this attack successful?

Most user-accessible APIs usually don't include the capabilities necessary for efficient testing. Take regression test suites for example; these are typically run on an application after any significant change is made to the code, which could be every week, every day, or even more often. Without adding testing hooks and APIs to the application for automating regression tests, this task would be unmanageable. Some tests target features that have nothing to do with security, but access to these features through user APIs may require additional security-related checks that would slow testing.

Test APIs are usually included in applications with the intention of removing them before release. In practice, though, schedules often run late, and test APIs become so integrated into the testing process that they are sometimes left in the released product. In the worst cases, some functional code actually *depends* on this test code, and when test APIs are removed, functional code might fail.

HOW to determine whether security is compromised

Security is compromised whenever test APIs can be used to bypass normal security controls. Look for username and password prompts while accessing specific types of data or application features through the user interface. Once these "protected" resources are identified, see how testing tools access them. This may involve getting into the internals of test scripts and tracing the steps that they take to access sensitive data. Uncovering a vulnerability may involve a step-by-step comparison between controls through UI access and through test APIs.

HOW to conduct this attack

Holodeck is the key to this attack. The idea is to watch the application under Holodeck for suspicious library loads. Test libraries may be loaded when the application first starts or may not load until a testing tool prompts the application. You probably already had a good deal of experience using Holodeck to look for suspicious libraries in Chapter 2. The knowledge you gained about your application's dependencies there will be very helpful during this attack also.

The more you know about which libraries your application uses and for what purpose, the better able you will be to identify problems. Talk to developers. Take the list of libraries you found with Holodeck to them and work out which libraries provide legitimate services to the application.

Here are some steps to try:

1. Gather any in-house testing tools, scripts, harnesses, and the like.
2. Open up your application in Holodeck and watch these testing tools run. Automated regression suites can be especially revealing.
3. Look for library loads and make a note of which libraries load and when.
4. Talk to developers to determine whether they can identify which libraries provide legitimate services to the application.

If you follow these steps, at the very least you will become intimately familiar with your application's dependencies (which will make the attacks in Chapter 2, Attacking Software Dependencies, that much more effective). There is a fair chance, though, that you may uncover a weakness in your application from test instrumentation.

ATTACK 11 Connect to all ports

WHEN to apply this attack

A port is a method of organizing network traffic that is received or sent from a machine, so that different types of data can be transmitted simultaneously. When a port is "open," the operating system is "listening" for data through that interface. Applications commonly open ports to send data across the network. However, an open port is not automatically a secure conduit for communication. Without proper measures taken by application developers, an open port is a welcome mat for a hacker attempting to gain unauthorized access to a system.

Port numbers range from 0 to 65535. Some special ports are used by default by most operating systems for specific types of communication. Ports 1 through 1023 are controlled by the IANA (Internet Assigned Number Authority) and correspond to the most common types of data transfer. Table 4.2 lists some commonly used port numbers for specific

TABLE 4.2 Some of the most commonly used ports

Port Number	Service	Description
7	Echo	
21	FTP	File Transfer Protocol control port
23	Telnet	Telnet access port
25	SMTP	Simple Mail Transfer Protocol
53	DNS	Domain Name Server
70	Gopher	
79	Finger	
80	HTTP	Hyper Text Transfer Protocol. This is the port your Web browser connects to a full stop
107	Rtelnet	Remote Telnet Service
110	POP3	Post Office Protocol–Version 3
119	NNTP	Network News Transfer Protocol
194	IRC	Internet Relay Chat

types of data. *Note: port numbers greater than 1023 are usually application specific and should be meticulously investigated.*

WHAT faults make this attack successful?

There are many reasons why an application may decide to open a port. The problem with opening application-specific ports is that the application may not properly restrict data through this channel. It is common for ports to be opened for application data (such as dynamic software updates) but to be completely unconfigurable by the user. In these cases, the user is at the mercy of the developer's implemented security controls. Testers are responsible for making sure developers did their job.

HOW to determine whether security is compromised

This can be difficult. Uncovering unsafe behavior requires you to perform some unauthorized action remotely. Most of the time, just opening a port unnecessarily can create the potential for a security vulnerability. As a security tester, you need to know which ports your application uses and when. In practical terms, this means having the right tools to assess the impact of an open port. A custom port scanner is included with this book, and its use will be discussed in the next section.

HOW to conduct this attack

Included on the CD-ROM that ships with this book is a port scanner that will check your system for open ports and capture error messages from ports that appear to be closed. A good starting point would be to accept the default configuration of the scanner, so that it checks for all open ports and creates a list of those that are open and those that appear to be closed but have returned nonstandard error messages that may be revealing.

Take a look at Figure 4.1, which shows our port scanner in its default configuration. The scanner can be used to detect both open ports and those that return revealing error messages from a machine. The scanner provides output in HTML format which is easily readable. If the Scan and View Output box is checked, the application will open the file in Microsoft's Internet Explorer if present on the system.

Figure 4.2 shows the results of a machine scan in IE. There are two things to look out for in implementing this procedure. The most obvious are open ports that are listed first in the output, as shown in Figure 4.2. When a port is open, it is your job as a tester to determine which application is communicating through that port, why, and the implications of that open communication channel on security. It may turn out that the port was not opened by your application, but you must nevertheless ensure that malicious data received through this channel cannot make its way into your application.

The second thing to look out for is a nonstandard error message. Some applications open ports and attempt to conceal the fact that they are open. These ports may send out custom error messages in response to attempts to connect to them. A nonstandard error message is a sign that one of the two situations applies to that port. These situations bear further investigation. One way to pursue it further is to go back to the scanner and choose the suspicious port as the sole port to be scanned. One of the options is to scan from a range of ports. Some applications only respond to network packets from certain ports on the sending machine. You can pick either a range of ports to scan from or choose the entire range. Next, examine the output and carefully review messages returned from the scan. You may uncover an open port that is not documented or that allows malicious data to enter the system.

An interesting example of a dangerous open-port vulnerability was found on WinGate 2.1, a popular network connection-sharing application for Windows 95 and 98[2]. WinGate allows users to share a connection to the

FIGURE 4.1 The FITScanner Port Scanner. From this screen we can pick a machine to target, assess which ports are open, and identify any revealing information from the errors returned from closed ports.

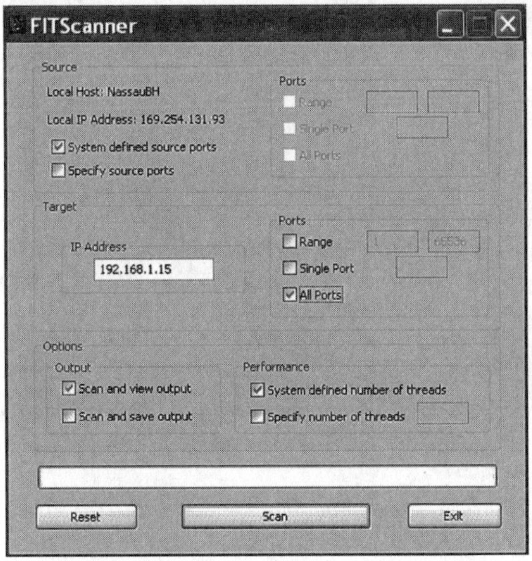

---

[2]This bug was reported at http://www.ntbugtraq.com/default.asp?pid=36&sid=1&A2=ind9904&L=NTBUGTRAQ&P=R340

Internet or some other network through a single machine. This would allow, for example, a network of a few machines to all use an active connection that one machine (perhaps one with a modem) has to the Internet. The vulnerability lies with the application's Logfile service, which allows a user to remotely view the application logs. Logfile essentially opens a Webserver on port 8010, which, by default, allows an attacker to access the contents of the drive hosting the service. For example, if the service was running on the server addressed by break_it.com, then an attacker could access the drive by typing into the address bar of a browser

```
http://www.break_it.com:8010/
```

This vulnerability has since been fixed in later releases, but it hammers home an important point: as testers, we must know which ports our applications use and the impact of these open channels on the system.

FIGURE 4.2	The scanner displays its results of a making scan in HTML format, which can be viewed with many applications, including Internet Explorer.

FITScanner Scan Report - Microsoft Internet Explorer

Address C:\Program Files\FIT\FITScanner\Scan.html

FITScanner on Local Host: NassauBH
Source IP address: 169.254.131.93
Target IP address: 127.0.0.1
Scan type: LOCAL HOST
Source Port Range: System defined
Target Port Range: from 1 to 2000

SUCCESSFUL SCANS

TARGET PORT	STATUS	SOURCE PORT
110	OPEN	65445
135	OPEN	65469
641	OPEN	65376
1024	OPEN	65461
1025	OPEN	65461
1037	OPEN	65472

NON-STANDARD ERRORS

TARGET	STATUS	SOURCE	ERROR

ATTACK **12**   Fake the source of data

WHEN to apply this attack

Some data is trusted implicitly, based on its source; for example, applications tend to accept values from sources like the OS with minimal scrutiny. Some sources should be trusted (in fact they *must* be trusted) for the application to function—sources such as configuration commands from an authenticated administrator. Problems arise when the trust an application extends to a particular source is not commensurate with the checks it makes to ensure that data is indeed from that source. This attack focuses on ensuring that applications take the proper precautions to verify the source of data, and that even when verified, the level of trust the application extends to that source is appropriate. This attack is applicable whenever the application accepts data from multiple sources and processes that data differently based on its perceived source.

WHAT faults make this attack successful?

The main problem is that trust is extended solely based on *identification* without being coupled with *authentication*. These two terms are often confused: Identification is the act of saying who you are. Authentication is *proving* that you are who you *say* you are. An example would be a username and password. The username is how an individual identifies himself or herself to the system. Passwords authenticate that users are whom they say they are. These two actions tend to get confused in software, and sometimes data is accepted as from a legitimate source based on circumstance. It's like someone walking up to a cigarette stand drinking a beer: although the vendor would normally ask the buyer for identification proving that they are 18 years old (the required age for purchasing cigarettes in the United States), the bottle of beer (which can only be purchased by someone 21 and over in the U.S.) may lead to the cigarettes being sold without bothering to verify the buyer's age. In this example, the beer serves as an informal form of identification; it says to the vendor that the holder is at least 21 years of age, which may be accepted without authentication (that is, a valid ID). Another example is a flaw in various UNIX applications that would determine identity based on the source IP address in a network packet. Such data is very easily spoofed, and should not be used to validate authenticity.

Software developers similarly suffer from these bad assumptions. When data arrives in the form that the application expects, the application may extend it some undeserved credibility. Especially suspect should be network data that can be poorly authenticated. The issue with network data is that if an application is expecting certain data, and if data is received in the expected form, it is unlikely that additional steps would be taken to verify its source.

HOW to determine whether security is compromised

Security is compromised whenever we can get the application to accept data or commands from an untrusted or unauthenticated source that passes itself off as legitimate.

HOW to conduct this attack

Follow these steps:

1. Think through the data your application receives through input channels.
2. For each type of data, try to determine which user is associated with it. A user could be an actual person, a process, or a location (file system, registry, IP address, etc.).
3. Try to determine the privileges and level of trust each user is entitled to.
4. From a less-privileged platform, try to alter the tag, field, property, etc., that identifies that data's source.

If you are restricted from performing a task as a certain user but can get the application to execute it anyway by impersonating a different user or data source, your attack has been successful.

An interesting example of this type of vulnerability was uncovered in Quake Server[3]. Quake is a popular multiplayer action game in which users can compete against other players via the network. Quake Server is used to host these games and can be set up by one or more of the individuals involved in a match. The server has a feature that allows an administrator to remotely send commands to the server with a password. Once authenticated, the administrator is able to execute arbitrary commands on the server. The vulnerability results from treating packets that appear to originate from ID Software (the makers of Quake) differently than packets from other locations. If a packet is received from the ID Software subnet (192.246.40.x) with password *tms,* the commands included in the packet would be executed by the server without the server questioning, or even monitoring, their actions. One can only speculate as to why such behavior was included in the product, but it created a severe vulnerability because anyone could craft such a packet and have full control over an affected machine. Quake relied solely on the source field of a packet and a weak static password to allow administrative control over the machine.

This attack is designed to weed out vulnerabilities such as these that are exploitable by spoofing the source of data.

---

[3]This vulnerability was originally reported by Mark Zielinski, and the advisory can be found at http://online.securityfocus.com/advisories/249.

ATTACK 13　Create loop conditions in any application that interprets script, code, or other user-supplied logic

WHEN to apply this attack

Some commands, when executed in isolation, are harmless. Imagine opening a Web browser and navigating to a Website that launches another window. This action by itself may be annoying, but it doesn't represent a threat to the end user. Now imagine that new window launching a third window, followed by another and another. Without some sanity checks by the browser, the system would become deadlocked.

This attack investigates these repeated actions: taking commands that are relatively benign and executing them over and over again to deny functionality to entitled users or processes.

WHAT faults make this attack successful?

Some actions are obviously dangerous. Allowing a highly restricted user to execute a format command on the local hard disk is something that OS developers would obviously want to prohibit. Similarly, there are many actions and commands that, in isolation, seem harmless. However, when these actions are combined with others, or can be forced to execute in a loop, they can have disastrous consequences. Trying to predict these consequences is exquisitely difficult; it's almost impossible to determine where to draw the line between legitimate use and a maliciously crafted sequence of actions. Loops form an especially difficult-to-protect-against subset of these problems.

HOW to determine whether security is compromised

Security compromises usually take the form of denial of service on a remote server. The goal is to make some feature unavailable to authorized users by forcing an application to consume computing resources by executing a loop. Look for application hangs and severe performance hits on the target system or application. If you can deny a legitimate user access to a resource, the attack was successful.

HOW to conduct this attack

Begin by finding out which, if any, user inputs get processed as more than just a string. Look for parsed values like HTML fields, and try to enter commands that automatically repeat. For example, take a look at the script below:

```
<SCRIPT LANGUAGE="VbScript">
On Error Resume Next
Dim a
Dim i
for i=1 to 100
Set a = CreateObject("Word.Application")
Next
</SCRIPT>
```

This script, if placed on a Website, will attempt to open 100 instances of Microsoft Word on the computer of anyone who browses to the site and is running an unpatched version of Microsoft's Internet Explorer[4]. This would undoubtedly hang or crash the client machine, thus implementing a pretty effective remote attack.

The key is to discover the set of commands that your application will process. In this example, the target was Internet Explorer. IE interprets many types of script and formatting commands. A good rule of thumb is to track the flow of data processed by your application and find data that is formatted or that can contain macros and embedded code. Once you have identified how that data is fed into the application, experiment with commands and sequences of commands that cause actions to occur over and over again.

ATTACK 14   Use alternate routes to accomplish the same task

WHEN to apply this attack

How many ways can you open a Microsoft Word® file in Windows XP? You could:

- Type the path in the Run dialog box.
- Double-click on the file's icon in an Explorer window.
- Type the path and file name in an Explorer window.

---

[4]This bug was first reported on bugtraq at http://online.securityfocus.com/archive/1/266712. The user is prompted asking whether or not to allow the ActiveX object (Word) to be created. No matter what the user's response, the Word objects are still created in memory.

- Type the path and file name in an Internet Explorer window.
- Select it from the My Recent Documents tab on the Start menu.
- Type the file name in the Open dialog box within Word.
- Etc., etc., etc.

There are many ways in which to accomplish this task, but whichever method we choose, we expect the same result: our document will be displayed and be ready to edit. Now imagine trying to implement a security control on that document. To be effective, we must anticipate every possible scenario and verify that each goes through our validation routine; this can be a daunting task for even the most experienced developer. Cases get missed, and the result is a route that circumvents security controls.

This attack is designed to help you think about the applications you test and explore all possible ways of accomplishing a task, not just typical user scenarios. The attack is widely applicable in GUI applications that are notorious for multiple-access routes to application features.

WHAT faults make this attack successful?

Software inherits many characteristics from its environment. The way users see and interact with an application in a GUI environment is governed by features of the OS. Imagine, for example, a simple text editor built from a template to include standard editing functions, including the ability to launch a new document by selecting a menu option. The developer may want to restrict the user from creating a new document window by removing this menu option. They may have forgotten, however, that this command is also accessible through a keyboard shortcut (commonly Ctrl-N in Windows). Another commonly forgotten feature that has many routes of access is copy-paste.

When developers use code templates or controls without understanding all the features they have built in, they may be creating undesirable functionality. These additional features can create routes to functionality that developers may not be aware of. If they miss even *one* of these pathways, securing all of the others is futile, because hackers will continue trying different approaches until they find one that works.

HOW to determine whether security is compromised

Security exploits found using this attack enable a user to perform restricted actions. A good way to identify problems is to consult user-help documentation and follow the steps that they list to perform a specific task. After you have gotten a feel for restrictions—places where you are asked to authenticate, grayed out buttons, and the like—compare these security measures with those you find when accessing the same feature or data through some under-used set of inputs. If there is even *one* check or restriction that can be bypassed, security is compromised.

HOW to conduct this attack

The best way to start is to think of some task that your software does that requires authentication or user privilege. Next, try to list all the possible ways you could accomplish that task. You may also find it fruitful to consider each individual building block for the task in question. Sometimes the task is restricted, but the individual building blocks are not; and they can be cobbled together to give users functionality they should not possess. Such "substitute functionality" exists in many applications and can be dangerous.

Here's an example that shows a very serious bug that we uncovered in Internet Explorer 6 on Windows XP using this attack[5]. Our target action was accessing email through Microsoft Exchange Server's Outlook Web Access interface. Normally, we would open IE and navigate to the Internet address of our Exchange server and be prompted for a user name and password (see Figure 4.3).

FIGURE 4.3   The user is asked to authenticate to access email through Outlook Web Access.

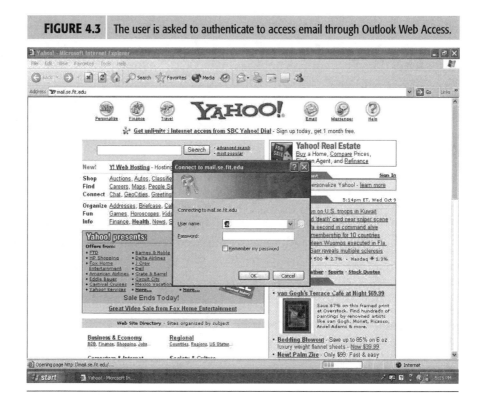

---

[5] This vulnerability was reported to the vendor and has been fixed.

We then asked the question: how else could we get IE to access our mail? After trying several combinations of Internet Explorer and Windows Explorer, we found a case in which user credentials are cached even after all instances of IE are terminated. The behavior occurs if you first open an IE window, then a Windows Explorer window. You can then type the Web address of the Exchange Server into the Explorer window, and because of the integration of Explorer and Internet Explorer, IE navigates to the page and correctly prompts for a password, as shown in Figure 4.4.

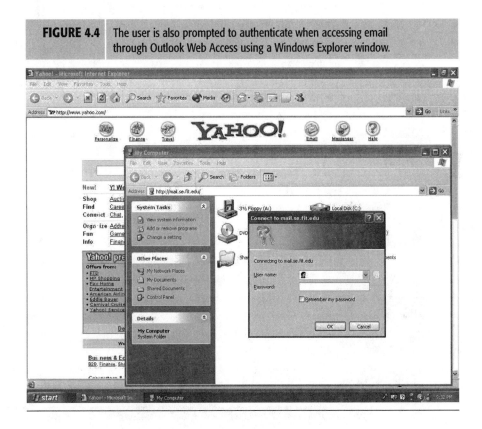

FIGURE 4.4 The user is also prompted to authenticate when accessing email through Outlook Web Access using a Windows Explorer window.

Both windows are then closed and the user now has the perception that they are logged out since all open IE windows have been closed. Indeed, if Internet Explorer is then launched, you are asked to authenticate before being allowed to read email. If you instead launch Windows Explorer, you can navigate to the Outlook Web Access site without being prompted for a password (Figure 4.5).

If you were to then click on any individual message, a password prompt appears, as shown in Figure 4.6. This can easily be subverted though by invoking the preview-pane window (Figure 4.7). This is a good example of substitute functionality, which we discussed earlier. The preview pane substitutes for viewing the message, and Windows Explorer substitutes for IE; both constitute dangerous new paths to restricted functionality by unauthorized users.

FIGURE 4.5   After both IE windows are closed, we launch a new Windows Explorer window and navigate to the Outlook Web Access page without being prompted for a password.

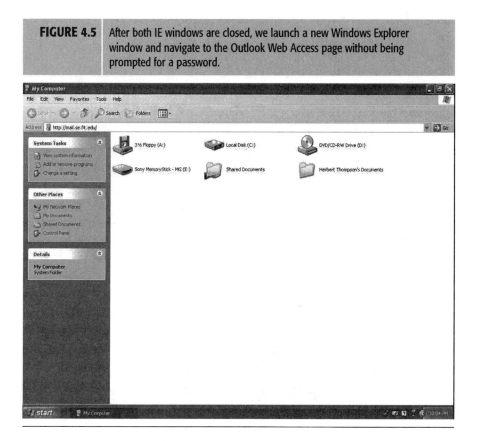

FIGURE 4.6   The unauthorized access to Outlook Web Access is then rectified if we try to view an email by double clicking on it.

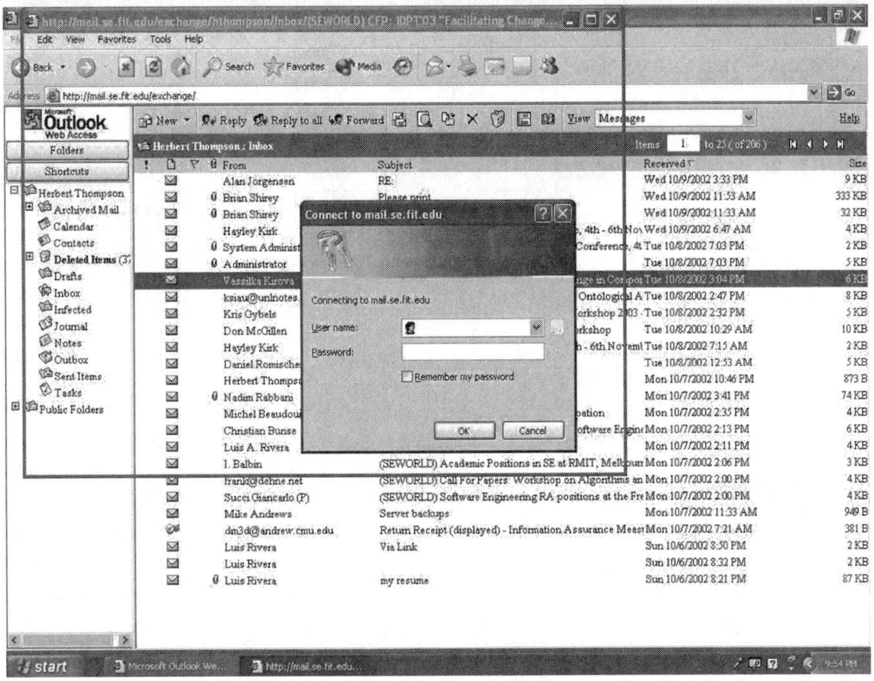

FIGURE 4.7   … or we could just open the preview pane.

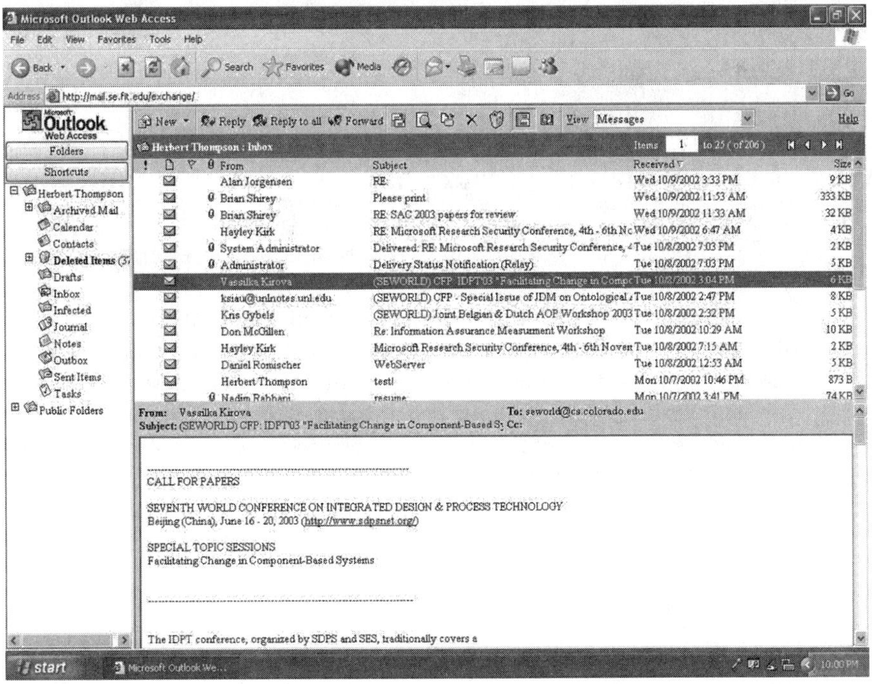

ATTACK **15** | Force the system to reset values

WHEN to apply this attack

This attack can be applied to all types of software. It is one of our favorites, because you don't really need to do anything; indeed, that's the whole point of the attack. Leave fields blank, click Finish instead of Next or just delete values. These types of actions force the application to provide a value where you haven't.

Establishing default values is a fairly intricate programming task. Developers have to make sure that variables are initialized before a loop is entered or before a function call is made. If this isn't done, then an internal variable might get used without being initialized. The result is often catastrophic.

Whenever a variable is used, it must first be assigned a legitimate value. Good programming practice is to assign a value to a variable as soon as it is declared in order to avoid these types of failures. In practice, though, programmers often assume that the user will provide a legitimate value in the course of the application's execution before the variable is used.

For security, the biggest concern is that default values and configurations can leave the software in an unsafe state. This attack is focused on forcing the application to use these default values and then assessing the vulnerabilities that these values produce. For example, take the installation of firewall software; many system administrators tend to leave application defaults in place, especially for obscure options. It is our job as testers to make sure that default configurations are secure.

WHAT faults make this attack successful?

Security testers need to check for two types of faults: variables that have illegal or nonexistent default values and default values and configurations that leave the software in an unsafe state.

Garbage default values occasionally pop up because developers rely on users to fill certain application fields. When user input is missing, the software is forced to revert to any default value that may have been coded. When a variable gets declared and then used before a value is assigned, the variable usually ends up taking some random value from a convenient memory block. This can lead to some perplexing and difficult-to-trace failures that may not easily reproduce. Some of these errors are caught at compile time or through the use of code scanning software, but many make it past these checks and to the consumer.

Although missing defaults are the easiest faults in this category to identify, insecure default configurations and values present the biggest security threat. These types of bugs are routinely missed or just plain ignored during testing because of a lack of clearly defined security requirements.

HOW to determine whether security is compromised

If an application is forced to use an invalid default value, it is likely to crash. This is certainly a quality problem, but from a security standpoint, we must ensure that the software cannot be forced into this state remotely and that the nonfunctioning application does not leave the system or data in a vulnerable state.

One of the more common and serious concerns with this class of vulnerability is that the application may have default values that leave it in an unprotected state. The general rule of thumb is that default settings should err on the side of restriction and caution. This is especially true for the more obscure options that users are unlikely to change, understand, or even know about.

HOW to conduct this attack

An interesting exercise is to step through any series of dialog boxes or wizards that your application may have and enter the minimal set of values that will allow you to continue and see what happens. This will force the application to use developer-assigned default values.

A common tactic used by developers is to gray out the Next and Finish buttons of a wizard until some critical data is entered into a field or an option is selected. Try entering a value and then deleting it. In some cases, even though this is the same state that did not allow you to continue earlier (when the field was blank by default), you may now be allowed to proceed, forcing the application to provide a value for the field.

By far the most common insecure default values are established at application installation. It is well known that both users and administrators routinely accept "recommended" and default configuration values. It is important to ensure that these values are appropriately secure and that you understand the implications of default and recommended configurations to the application, its host system, and user data. One effective method we have found is to look at each option individually and think through its implications with respect to the application's security. This seems simple enough, but remember that many defaults are set based on individual component configurations that are usually written by different developers or development groups. Few people in the organization have a "big picture" view of the application and of the implications of configuration decisions on other parts of the software. As testers, the burden falls on us to ensure that the result is an application that users can trust out of the box.

Summary of the Design Attacks: A Checklist for Battle

1. Try common default usernames and passwords anywhere your application requires authentication. Look for accounts that may have existed in previous versions of the application that are not documented in the current version.

2. Launch your application under Holodeck and look for libraries that are loaded by the application when automated test harnesses and suites are run. Try to isolate which libraries provide legitimate services to the application and which are used only for testing purposes.

3. Use the port scanner included with this book to determine which ports your application opens and when. Determine which data is being sent and received through these open ports.

4. Fake the source of data read by the application. Try to find out which data sources your application trusts, and then try to get it to accept data from an untrusted location by faking its source.

5. Find out where your application accepts user-supplied logic. Look for formatted text or script. Try to force the application into an infinite loop through user-supplied data remotely.

6. Explore alternate routes to functionality and data. Pay particular attention to tasks that may be restricted or require authentication and how you might take another route to access that feature or data.

7. Try empty values and other actions to force the application to supply default values. Evaluate the security implications of these default values or configurations.

Conclusion

The attacks in this chapter are aimed at software that was designed to be insecure. Obviously, no ethical developer would purposefully do such a thing. Unfortunately, the truth of the matter is that secure design is not a subject that has been well studied.

Books are beginning to appear on this subject, which is a good sign, but until such design techniques become common practice, you'll find these attacks very useful for identifying and isolating serious security design flaws.

Exercises

The exercises presented here are *constructed* to help you understand how design attacks can be applied to your application. Professional testers can use whichever application they are currently working with. When we teach these techniques at Florida Tech, we usually pick an application before the semester begins, and then students apply the attacks to this application. Students working on their own will ideally select an application with many inputs, some of which are delivered remotely.

Once you've selected your application, perform the following exercises:

1. Look through test scripts for your application and documentation for previous application versions; list all the accounts you find. Try these accounts on your application and document the results.

2. Watch your application run under Holodeck while test suites run. Make a list of the libraries your application loads. Do some research and write one sentence about the types of services that each library provides to the application.

3. Install the port scanner that came with this book. Run a complete scan on your system when your application is running and then again when it isn't. Note any discrepancies.

4. Note any information sources that your application may trust implicitly. How does your application identify data as coming from these sources?

5. Examine the strings that your application accepts and the files that it may read or display. Look for formatted text or script commands. Make a note of those that are treated as more than just text.

6. In the fields that you identified in Exercise 5, can a user implement a self-reference or access control-flow statements such as FOR or WHILE loops?

7. Determine which functions or scenarios require authentication or prevent users from completing a task. For each, write down one alternate scenario that you could use to access that feature or data.

8. Go through any wizards or options that your application has. For each field that requires user input, leave that field blank or delete the "suggested" values that your application fills in for you. Record your observations.

9. Use the answers from these exercises to launch this chapter's attacks against your application. Note your results.

References

1. M. Howard and D.C. LeBlanc, *Writing Secure Code*, 2nd ed. Seattle: Microsoft Press, 2002.

2. J. Viega and G.E. McGraw, *Building Secure Software*. Boston, MA: Addison Wesley, 2001.

CHAPTER 5
Attacking Implementation

A perfect design can still be made vulnerable by imperfect implementation. For example, the Kerberos authentication scheme is renowned as a well thought out and secure authentication scheme, yet the MIT implementation has had many serious security vulnerabilities in its implementation, most notably, buffer overruns. Indeed, we can ensure that every aspect of the design is secure and still produce an unsecure product. The problem is that security is not communicated well down the design hierarchy. Developers are usually given a list of requirements that emphasize which interfaces their component should extend to the rest of the application and the form of data that their component will receive. They are also given requirements for the computation to be performed on that data. However, specific requirements are seldom given as to exactly how that computation should be performed.

As an example, consider a simple function that reverses a string. The developer is given these requirements:

- The function will take one argument, a string of twenty characters.
- Its return value should also be a string of the same length with the characters in reverse order; that is, the last character of the string should be the first in the returned value.

These constitute a simple set of requirements for a simple function. From a security standpoint, though, many things can go wrong. First, consider the number of possible ways you could implement the code in this function. You could, among other things, do the following:

- Store the characters in an array and reverse the array.
- Store the characters in individual variables, read them in reverse order, and reassemble the results into a new string.
- Write the string out to a file, and then read it back in reverse order.
- Use some external library to reverse the string.

Each option will produce a "correct" function when seen from the perspective of the stated requirements. However, if there are some additional, unstated security concerns involved, such as the string being passed to the function containing highly sensitive data, then the option of writing the data out temporarily to a file is unacceptable.

Incomplete requirements such as those above are a common source of implementation vulnerabilities. This chapter presents techniques to expose many such failures in software.

ATTACK **16**   Get between time of check and time of use

WHEN to apply this attack

Data is at risk whenever an attacker can separate the functions that check security around a feature or a piece of data from the functions that actually access and use these features or data. The ideal situation would be to ensure that every time sensitive operations are performed, checks are made to guarantee that they will succeed securely. If too much time elapses between the time the data is checked and the time it is used, then the possibility of the attacker infiltrating such a transaction must be considered. It is the old "bait and switch" con applied to computing: Bait the application with legitimate information, and then switch that information with illegitimate data before it notices.

WHAT faults make this attack successful?

Some actions are not performed atomically (that is, instantaneously) and involve multiple steps. When some security-related checks are necessary for a particular action, there is sometimes a gap between the time that the application checks to see whether a particular action is authorized and the point at which it is actually performed. This attack is designed to exploit this time delay and penetrate the process between these two functions, with the goal being to force the application to perform some unauthorized action.

The main reason this delay between check and use is exploitable is that developers tend to think of a series of certain actions as being continuous. The mental timeline that a developer has for instructions rarely includes the possibility of some event interceding. This misconception leads to implementation errors in which security is checked only at the beginning of a series of actions rather than every time sensitive data is accessed. The ultimate goal for developers should be to have their code perform the security check immediately before a sensitive operation. Our task as testers is to ensure that this is the case.

HOW to determine whether security is compromised

Security is compromised if you can escalate your privilege over some part of the application or its data—that is, gain access to some information or functionality that you are not authorized for. Failures usually don't take the form of spectacularly obvious crashes; they are generally much more subtle. To recognize failure requires both domain expertise and knowledge about the specific privileges assigned to certain users, features, actions, and data. Unfortunately, the specification might not be very helpful here. The reason is that the specification is usually written as "the application will do x" rather than "the application will do x but not do y or z. . . ." You will need to consider in more depth the value of data and features and how accessing them could violate the confidentiality, integrity, or availability of your application.

HOW to conduct this attack

Begin by looking for gaps between when a privilege is checked and when it is used. This is definitely a "think outside of the box" situation, because for every chain of events, you must be wary of points at which that chain can be interrupted and whether such an interruption can lead to data being compromised.

To illustrate, let's take a look at a classic example. One of the more famous time-of-check-to-time-of-use bugs was found in xterm, a terminal emulation application under UNIX that runs as the omnipotent "root" user and thus has unrestricted access to the system. The application enables a user of the system to log all input and output to a file. If the user already has a log file, xterm checks the permissions on that file to ensure that the user has write-access privileges to it, and then appends the current log to the end of the file. Because any root process can write to any file on the system, the check is necessary to prevent an unauthorized user from using xterm to write to a protected system file. After this check has been made, the application then blissfully writes to the file and no longer checks permissions. The vulnerability here is that the user can delete the log file (which he or she has control over) *after* the application checks its permissions, and then bind, say, the system password file to its name. Because xterm runs as the root user, it can write to this system file, whereas the user may not have permission to do so. Unauthorized users can then, through xterm, create a root account for themselves by appending data to the password file and thus gain full access to the system

Here's the sequence of events:

1. Start xterm, giving it log file `decoy`
2. Xterm checks permissions on `decoy` and determines that the user has the right to write to it.
3. Delete the file `decoy`.
4. Using the `ln` command, link `decoy` to `/etc/passwd`
5. In the same xterm, turn logging on.

6. Because xterm has previously checked and established that it can write to `decoy`, it doesn't check again and appends log output to it.

7. Now the user can append data to the password file and create their own root account through the xterm application. Because xterm no longer bothers checking which file it is writing to, the user can exploit this and write to the system password file.

A good starting point for this attack is to make a list of all the actions that your application requires authentication to perform. Next, determine the actions that make up this task and determine which ones can be interrupted. Like the example just discussed, changing the path of an accessed file is usually a good place to begin looking.

ATTACK 17   Create files with the same name as files protected with a higher classification

WHEN to apply this attack

Some files enjoy special privileges based on their location. For example, take dynamic link libraries (dlls). These libraries are used to perform certain tasks and are loaded by the application either at startup or when needed. Depending on where these libraries are located in the directory structure, a user with restricted privileges may not be allowed to alter them or write to the directory that contains them. Attackers can take advantage of the fact that these libraries are usually loaded by name, without any further checks to make sure that they are indeed the desired files. This can be exploited by creating a file with the same name and placing it in a directory the user *does* have access to that the application may search first.

A related issue is that some files are given special privileges based solely on their names. This is a common phenomenon, especially with antivirus software that operates using a complex mesh of filtering rules based on filenames and their extensions.

This attack will target both behaviors and is applicable any time an application makes execution or privilege decisions based on filename.

WHAT faults make this attack successful?

One of the most common sources of vulnerability we have found has to do with the search order of applications for libraries. Applications that run in Windows have a very specific sequence of directories that they search when looking for a library. When a specific library is requested on versions of Windows prior to Windows XP SP1 and Windows Server 2003, the application first searches in the same directory as the executable for the library. If it is found there, then it is loaded without any further checks. If the library is not found, Windows searches in the `%system%\system32` directory, where most applications and the OS store their libraries. On most Windows machines, only a highly privileged user can write to the `System32` directory, making the replacement of certain dlls impossible. On the other hand, many users with lower privilege levels can write to the directory that contains the target executable. We have discovered a number of privilege-escalation problems in which an application runs with greater privileges than its user; thus if a user can get a privileged application to use a well-crafted bogus library, then the user can execute commands at the higher privilege of the application.

Another class of vulnerabilities results from files being treated as special cases based on their name. The file AUX in the Windows operating system is a good example of this. Nearly any combination of letters (of reasonable length) can come together to create a valid Windows filename. The filename AUX is an exception to this rule. AUX, along with LPT1, COM1, and others, are used to represent devices in Windows. Many applications that have the ability to save files can easily be broken by naming the target file one of these identifiers. Some applications however, such as Microsoft's WordPad, are aware of these peculiarities and respond appropriately when we try to open the file C:\AUX, as shown in Figure 5.1. Others, such as Microsoft's Internet Explorer 5 do not (see Figure 5.2).

FIGURE 5.1 When WordPad attempts to open the file C:\AUX, it properly recognizes it as a device name.

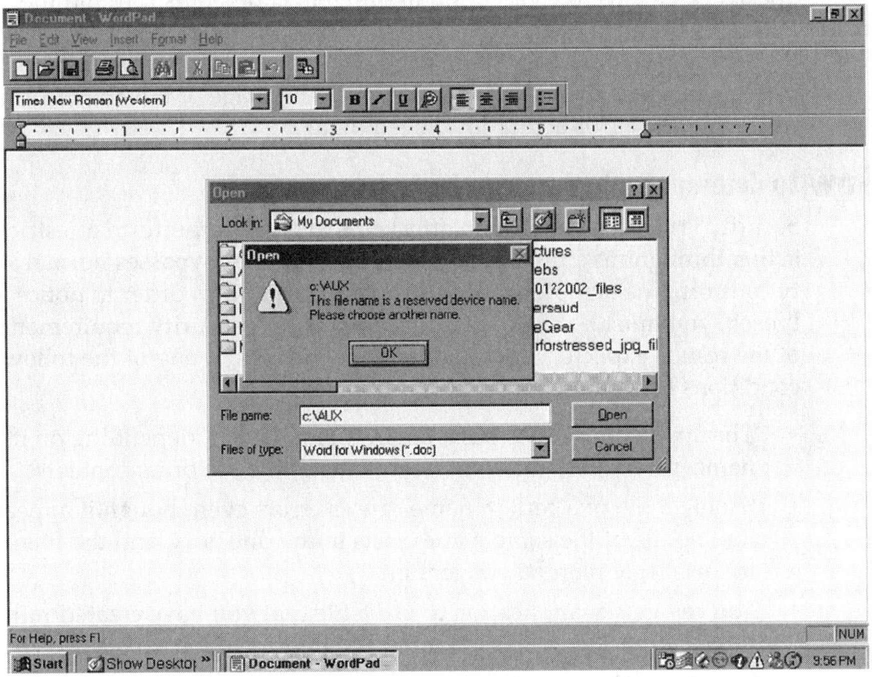

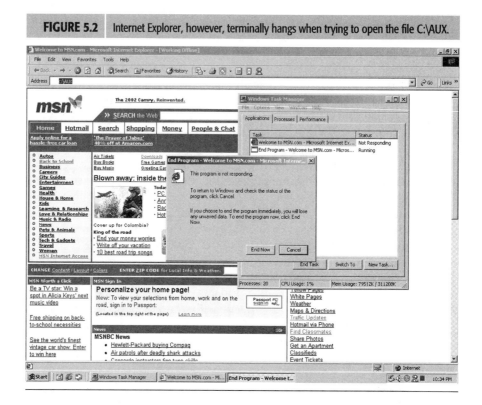

FIGURE 5.2 | Internet Explorer, however, terminally hangs when trying to open the file C:\AUX.

Special cases force the execution of different code paths through the software. Where filenames are concerned, a file may be given special privileges (or restrictions) based solely on its name. From a security point of view, we must ensure that an attacker cannot take advantage of this to perform restricted actions or access privileged data.

HOW to determine whether security is compromised

Security is compromised if an attacker is allowed to perform a restricted action through manipulating or creating a file that bypasses normal security controls. The symptoms of this can vary widely. In order to notice a breach, you must be aware of your application's security requirements and of the results expected from a given set of actions. If any of the following conditions hold, there might be a problem:

- The application processes a file in various ways, depending on its name, that causes different treatments of the file or its contents.

- Saving a file of a certain name causes errors even though it appears that no file of the same name exists in the directory, and the filename follows legal naming conventions.

- You can get an application to use a file that you have created rather than another file with the same name that you don't have access to; for example, placing a dll in the application's directory—a directory which a restricted user may have access to—and forcing the application to use this library instead of one stored in %system%\System32, a directory which a restricted user is unlikely to have access to.

HOW to conduct this attack

Pick a feature in your application that interacts with the file system. Think through the files and file types that this feature may try to read.

For example, take a look at the folder appearance functions that are included in Windows 98 and above. Users can change the appearance of a folder by adding a file called desktop.ini to that directory. Microsoft Developer Network (MSDN) online[1] states that the commands shown in Figure 5.3 are necessary "if you want to use a custom Folder.htt template." Thus we can reason that the desktop.ini file is processed differently from other files in a folder. Desktop.ini is read to determine basic properties of the folder and states that the file "Folder.htt" provides further formatting information. We now have two files to target.

Let's consider what would constitute a security breach in this situation. Because we are altering folders on the local machine, it would appear that there is little threat. However, consider the issue of privilege escalation and how this might be achieved: A normal user is allowed to alter folders that he or she creates. If we can entice a privileged user to browse a folder that automatically executes commands by simply viewing the contents of that folder (which would normally be considered harmless, especially on the local machine), then a less-privledged user can execute commands at the same privilege level as the user who is browsing the folder.

FIGURE 5.3	Desktop.ini is a special file in Windows that can be placed in a folder that alters that folder's appearance. The file depicted here tells the operating system that additional formatting information is contained in the file "Folder.htt," which can execute a script and which is launched automatically when the folder is browsed with the default Windows settings.

```
desktop.ini - Notepad
File  Edit  Format  View  Help

[ExtShellFolderViews]
Default={5984FFE0-28D4-11CF-AE66-08002B2E1262}
{5984FFE0-28D4-11CF-AE66-08002B2E1262}={5984FFE0-28D4-11CF-AE66-08002B2E1262}

[{5984FFE0-28D4-11CF-AE66-08002B2E1262}]
PersistMoniker=file://Folder.htt
```

---

[1]http://msdn.microsoft.com/library/default.asp?url=/library/en-us/shellcc/platform/shell/programmersguide/shell_int/shell_int_extending/webview.asp

The format file "Format.htt" has the ability to execute a script. Through such a script, we can execute commands that are triggered by simply browsing the folder[2]. All we need to do is create a batch file to execute (we created one called boom.bat) and then invoke it from script code in "Format.htt." Figure 5.4 shows the result when a user browses to our malicious folder.

Closely observing results and reasoning about how file data can be used maliciously is the key to this attack. Looking for subtle (and not so subtle) differences in how various files are processed will give clues as to which files can be crafted to compromise security.

FIGURE 5.4 When we browse to our folder as a web page (the default) the malicious Folder.htt file launches boom.bat. If we can entice a privileged user—such as an administrator—to browse this folder, we can execute arbitrary commands on the system at the same privilege as the browsing user.

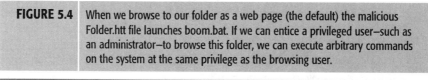

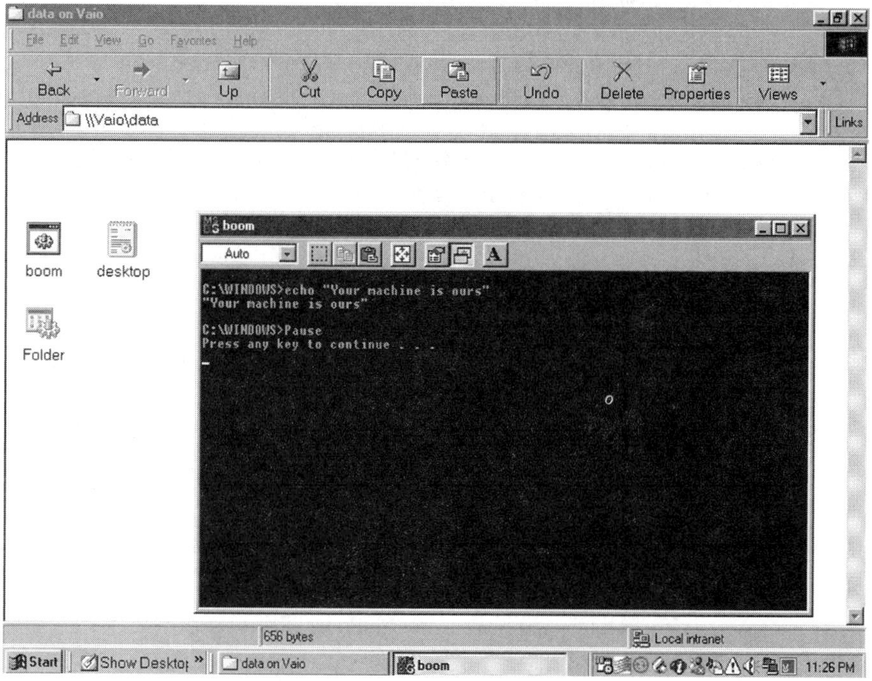

---

[2]This bug was originally found by Georgi Guninski, and the bug report can be found at http://www.sumthin.nu/archives/ntbt/Aug_2000/msg00016.html

ATTACK 18 Force all error messages

WHEN to apply this attack

Error messages are used to convey information to a user. Their purpose is to alert a user to some improper or disallowed action that may have been attempted. Our goal in this attack is to try to force the range of error messages that the application can display.

Those of you who read the original *How to Break Software* book may remember this attack. In that book, our focus was to think through the possible illegal values that could be entered into a field. By trying to cause error messages, you are actually covering the range of bad input to the application and testing its robustness to that data; an example would be trying to enter a negative value into a "number of siblings" Web field. Obviously, this is an illegal value, but by trying to force the application to display an error message indicating this, we are actually testing the application's ability to appropriately handle illegal input. The goal is to find a situation that is not handled appropriately; that is, no error message is displayed, and the application attempts to process the bad value.

For security, attempting to enter illegal values can be especially fruitful. We have three underlying motivations here:

1. An improper value that is not caught may be processed by the application and may result in a crash. This can be a denial-of-service concern if that data can be entered remotely or read through a file.

2. Computation on an improper value that is not caught may allow us to perform some illegal action. A good example of this would be an online florist that allows users to enter a tip or gratuity amount for the delivery person into a field. Forcing error messages in this case may lead us to enter a negative value in this field. It is likely that this gratuity amount would be added internally to other charges to create the final bill. If no checks are performed on the value from the gratuity field, a user may be able to give himself or herself an arbitrary discount on the order that may go unnoticed.

3. If an error message is displayed, it may contain information that is revealing to the attacker.

This attack is designed to address all three concerns.

WHAT faults make this attack successful?

Writing error cases and filters on data is itself very error prone and often poorly done in practice. One reason is that the normal development process is focused on adding functionality. The market pushes for features, and competition often forces release as soon as possible; as a result, managers push for functionality, and the sooner the better. This means that error handlers are often postponed in favor of complete functionality.

Error handlers are usually added after testers have broken functionality, and this can lead to a host of problems. The first and most obvious is that some vulnerabilities that are not explored by testers or thought of by developers get missed. This opens the door for input that can be used to exploit application logic, user data, or the system.

Another problem stems from the fact that error handlers may be written at different times to handle similar data; for example, take the process of logging into a system: One code path is taken when the user enters a valid username. This code path proceeds to check whether the password entered matches the one on record. If it does not, error message *A* is returned. Now consider the case when a user enters a username that is not a valid account. In this case, error message *B* is returned immediately. One problem could be that the error messages *A* and *B* may not have been written at the same time or by the same developer and may be subtly different. An attacker can exploit this by entering a string into the username field of a log-in prompt and observing which error message appears. If message *A* pops up, the attacker knows that they have a valid account and can write a script that tries alphanumeric combinations and get a list of all valid accounts on the system. A good example of this is included in the "how to conduct this attack" section of this attack.

HOW to determine whether security is compromised

There are two types of potential compromises that can be exposed through this attack. The first is that the application or the system may be breached by malicious data. For data that is accepted on a server from a remote user, allowing input that causes an application on the server to hang or crash is certainly a security concern. For noncrashing outcomes, you need to carefully examine how internal data or computation is affected by bad data entering the system.

The second, though less obvious, vulnerability is that sensitive data may be revealed by error messages. This may be true of a single message (in which sensitive data like internal machine names or path information is exposed explicitly) or of a series of messages (in which sensitive information can be inferred by comparing the differences in error messages).

HOW to conduct this attack

There are two approaches. The first is to test an application's robustness to erroneous input. The second is to review the error messages that result and ensure that they do not reveal any sensitive information that may be useful to an attacker. Therefore, for each type of illegal input we must ensure that the bad data is properly filtered and that any resulting error messages do not reveal any vulnerabilities.

Four general properties of input data to consider when trying to force an error message are described in the following subsections:

Input Length

By entering values that are longer than the application's data expectations, you can usually force an error message. If no error message is raised, then either that data is being truncated internally, the input you entered is not long enough, or the application does not respond proactively to long input. The second and third cases are the most interesting and may mean that the threat of a buffer overflow exists (see Chapter 3 for specific techniques for uncovering buffer overflows).

Input Type

Another good way to cause an error message is to enter input of a different type than was expected; for example, enter negative values, letters, or decimal numbers in fields that ask for whole-number values.

Boundary Values

Look for upper and lower limits of legal data values and choose values just above or below these limits. Good examples are fields that require positive integers. Sometimes these values may be used later in an internal computation. Many times the number 0 can force the application to behave strangely when used in computations. Developers may put checks on incoming data with the rule:

```
If (x<0) then goto error
```

when what they intended to write was:

```
If (x≤0) then goto error
```

The simple mistake of using a less-than sign rather than a less-than-or-equal sign can wreak havoc on future computations involving the value of x.

Another interesting set of inputs to try with numeric data is to attempt to underflow or overflow respectively the minimum or maximum value that the variable can store. This is different from entering long strings; here we take advantage of the fact that some variables are only equipped to handle integers up to a certain size. Try values near the boundaries of typical integer variables. Table 5.2 shows some typical boundary values for many compiled C and C++ applications.

Mishandling values beyond a variable's boundary can potentially be used to deny service if the data is read from a remote or untrusted user.

TABLE 5.1   Typical value ranges for integer data types in C and C++, arguably the most commonly used development languages for commercial software. These values may vary depending on the compiler and architecture used. Interesting test cases are at variable boundaries, such as those found in this table.

Variable Type	Bytes	Lower Bound	Upper Bound
signed short	2	−32767 or −32768	32767
unsigned short	2	0	65535
signed int	2	−32767 or −32768	32767
unsigned int	2	0	65535
signed long	4	$(1-2^{31})$ or (-2^{31})	$2^{31}-1$
unsigned long	4	0	$2^{32}-1$
signed long long	8	$(1-2^{63})$ or (-2^{63})	$2^{63}-1$
unsigned long long	8	0	$2^{64}-1$

Usernames, Machine Names, and Passwords

Some applications respond differently to legitimate usernames, passwords, and machine names as opposed to ones that do not exist. The danger is that an attacker can infer sensitive information based on the difference in error messages that result from valid or invalid accounts and machine names. To illustrate, let's consider a vulnerability that was uncovered in SAMBA, a popular file-sharing utility for Linux and UNIX. The vulnerability was in SAMBA's Web-management console, SWAT. Users can access SWAT through a browser by typing in the URL of the server and the appropriate port number (901 by default), as shown in Figure 5.5, which also shows a log-in attempt using an account that does not exist on the server. The result is the error message of Figure 5.6. Next take a look at Figure 5.7, which depicts the result of an attempt to log in to SWAT using a valid username (chosen by us to be "valid") but with an incorrect password. The result is the error message of Figure 5.8. Look carefully at the differences between the error messages in Figures 5.6 and 5.8. The messages are different, which indicates that there is some characteristic of the entered data that caused two different code paths to be executed. An attacker can exploit this difference in errors by using brute force to compile a list of legitimate user accounts.

As testers, we must ensure that an attacker is not given access to sensitive information that may give them a tactical advantage when conducting their attacks. It is important to scrutinize all error messages carefully and look for explicitly revealed information and for information that can be inferred by comparing multiple error messages.

FIGURE 5.5	We attempt to log in to SWAT, SAMBA's management console with a nonexistent account name.

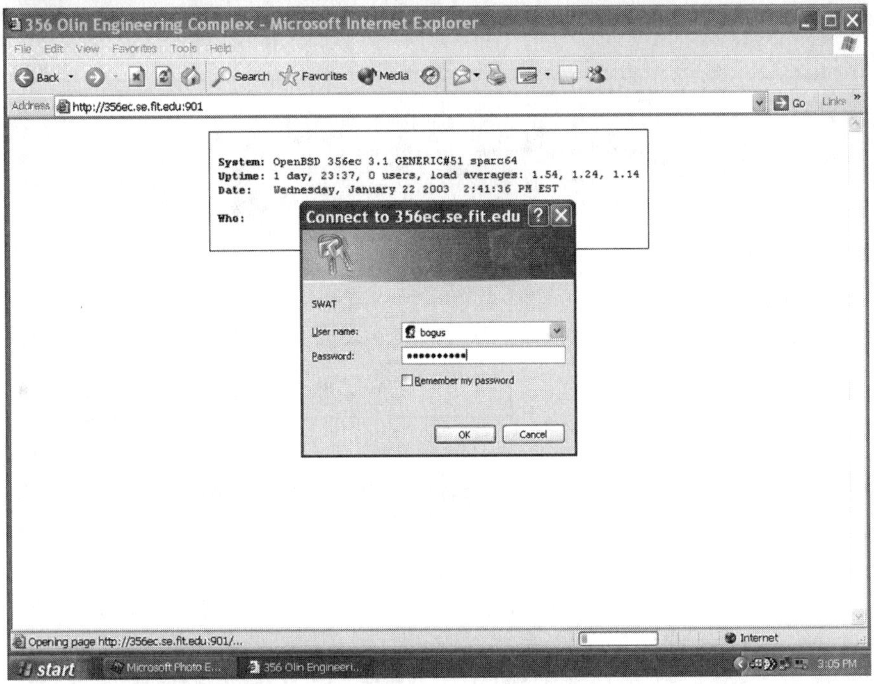

FIGURE 5.6	An invalid account name raises the error message shown here.

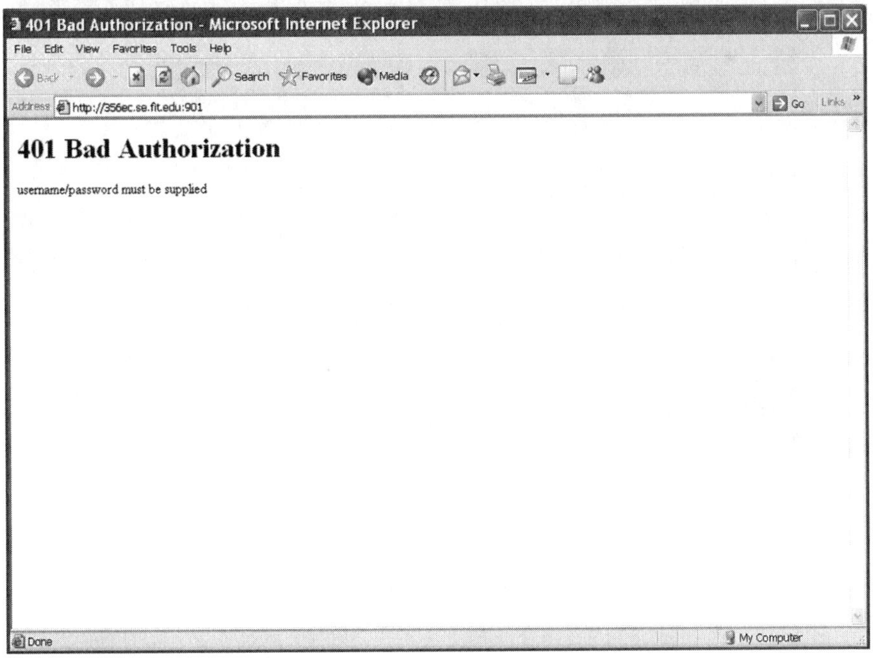

FIGURE 5.7	Next, we try to log in using a valid account name with an invalid password.

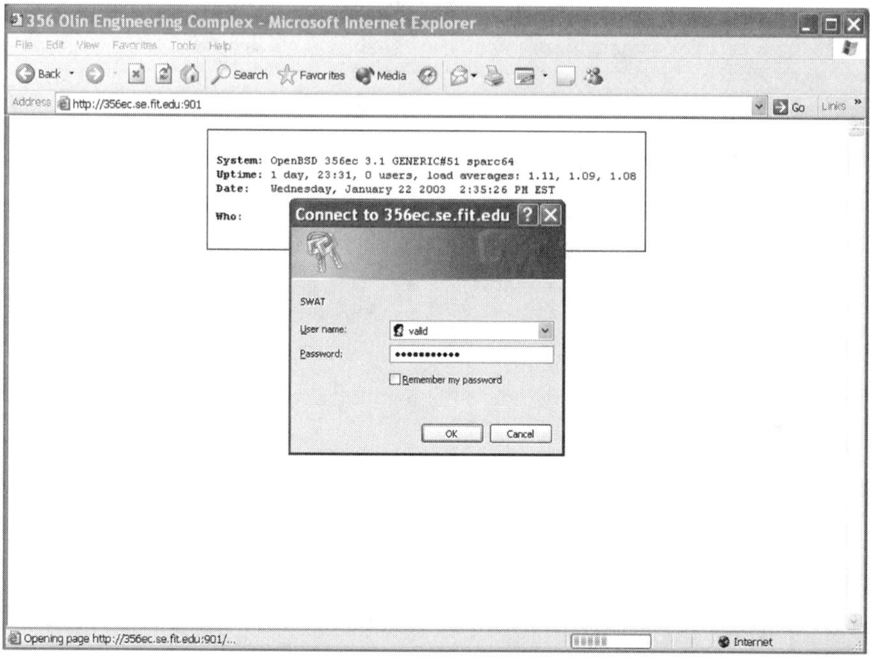

FIGURE 5.8	The valid account name with a bad password results in the error message shown here. Comparing this with the error message raised by using an *invalid* account name shows that they are different. An attacker can therefore tell the difference between a valid and an invalid account and, using brute-force techniques, can create a list of all valid account names on a system.

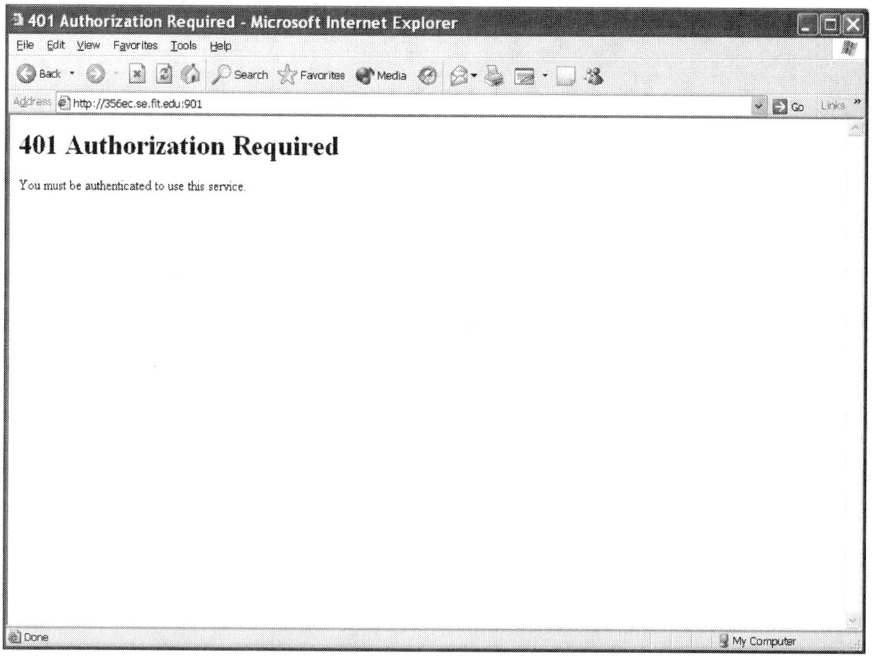

ATTACK **19** | Use Holodeck to look for temporary files and screen their contents for sensitive information

WHEN to apply this attack

Applications routinely write data to the file system, which can store both persistent (permanent) data and also temporary data. Temporary files can be created to transfer data between components or to hold data that may be either too large to hold in memory or too inefficient to keep there. If this data (CD keys, encryption keys, passwords, or other personal data) is sensitive, then the mechanism for storing this data and access points to this data need to be investigated. Testers, especially security testers, must be aware of when, where, and how the application accesses file-system data. To be effective, we must identify which data should not be exposed to other potential users of the system.

After sensitive data has been identified, we must find creative ways to gain insecure access to it. It is important to keep in mind that software lives in a multiuser, networked world, and just because our software created a file and deleted it doesn't mean that those operations went unnoticed by prying third parties. Our primary observation tool for this attack is Holodeck, which can monitor the application for file-writes and log these behaviors so that we can sift through them. Holodeck can tell us the *when, how* and *where* of every file access an application makes. It's up to us to investigate *what* was written and whether this data is supposed to be secret.

WHAT faults make this attack successful?

Temporary files are a convenient way to store data. This is particularly true when large amounts of data are being accessed or when an application needs to retain information between executions. Cookies are a good example of small files that hold persistent data between executions. Cookies usually hold user preferences, transaction data, and information about a Web application's "state." Web developers usually work on an implicit assumption that cookies will not be viewed or altered by the user or will not be viewed by a different user or web site. This leads to sensitive information (such as personal data, login information, shopping habits, and other data) being stored in plaintext in a cookie on the client's machine.

Another reason applications create temporary files is to free up memory for some other use. Vulnerabilities here stem from the assumption that data will not be read from the file, especially if that file will only exist on the disk for a very short period of time. Many encryption and decryption schemes for digital rights management are cracked because applications create decrypted versions of the files temporarily on the disk. This is especially true of any audio or digital media in which on-the-fly decryption in memory may cause poor playback quality but decrypting the file first to disk, playing the decrypted file, and then deleting it means that the playback will be smooth.

HOW to determine whether security is compromised

Exposing sensitive application or user data to a file system that is readily accessible by potential adversaries is certainly a security concern. It is critical that you understand which application data is sensitive and determine whether and when it gets exposed. By searching files that were identified using Holodeck, we can determine whether sensitive data is resident in the file system. It is also important to scrutinize these files and ensure that even if sensitive data is not exposed explicitly, characteristics of that data cannot be inferred from the information that was written out to the file system.

HOW to conduct this attack

This is a very straightforward attack. For Windows applications, follow these steps:

1. Identify which application and system information is considered sensitive. Thinking through data-exposure scenarios will allow you to conduct a more focused search when you start viewing temporary files.

2. Launch your application under Holodeck.

3. Watch for calls to all the incarnations of the Windows function CreateFile (CreateFileA, CreateFileW, etc.) and similar file operations, as shown in Figure 5.9.

4. You can pause the application's execution using Holodeck to view these temporary files before the application has a chance to delete them.

5. Open these files and screen their contents. You should be on the lookout for sensitive data that can be read by others and also data that can be manipulated by an attacker while stored on the file system and that may then be used by the application, which would assume that data to be trustworthy.

Following are two good examples, one from Windows and one from UNIX, that illustrate how temporary file vulnerabilities can manifest and how they can be found.

The first was discovered in RDISK, a utility in Windows NT that is "used to create an Emergency Repair Disk (ERD) in order to record machine state information as a contingency against system failure."[3]

---

[3]MSDN Online http://ww.microsoft.com/technet/treeview/default.asp?url=/technet/security/bulletin/MS00-004.asp

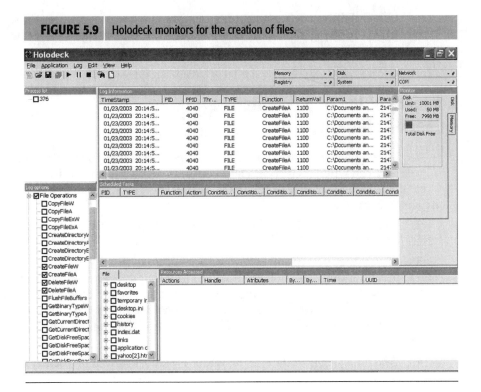

FIGURE 5.9 Holodeck monitors for the creation of files.

RDISK creates a file called $$hive$$.tmp, which contains a complete enumeration of the registry, which it first places in a directory and then deletes when it has finished using it. The temporary file is created with universal-read permission, meaning that even a highly restricted user could read its contents. The registry contains very security-sensitive information, and typically only administrators have access to certain values stored there. This vulnerability means that an attacker who has only restricted user privileges could run an application that watches for the temporary file and captures its contents. Such a vulnerability could have easily been uncovered by monitoring the utility for file writes.

A second vulnerability was uncovered in Pine 4.3, a popular email client in UNIX and Linux. Under certain configurations[4] when a user creates an email message, that message exists as a temporary file in a directory that is universally accessible. An attacker can exploit this in two ways:

- Most obviously, an attacker can simply read the file and gain access to the information contained in the outgoing message.

- Even more deviously, the user can replace this file just before it is sent so that the victim sends an email of the attacker's design rather than the original, intended one.

---

[4]See http://online.securityfocus.com/achive/1/150150 for more details.

Vulnerabilities such as these demonstrate the need to scrutinize files created by an application to ensure that sensitive information cannot be read or modified.

Summary of the Implementation Attacks: A Checklist for Battle

1. Identify any actions your application performs that have a time lapse between when security is checked for an action or data and when that privilege is actually used. Try to exploit this gap to escalate the privilege level of a user.

2. Some files are granted special permission based solely on their name or extension. Identify these files and replace them with malicious files.

3. Ensure that you see all error messages at least once by applying invalid input. Think of any invalid input that developers may have missed. Watch for two things: odd application behavior with no error raised and error messages that reveal sensitive data such as machine names, configurations, and other information that could be used by an attacker.

4. Watch the application execute under Holodeck, and look for temporary files. Examine their contents for sensitive information.

Conclusion

Incomplete requirements lead to insecure implementations. This is an undisputable fact and unfortunately reflects the current state of the practice in software engineering. Beyond the requirements problem, though, is the fact that developers are only human and therefore make mistakes. Functions get implemented incorrectly, and the result can be compromised data and functionality. The attacks presented in this chapter are designed to expose many of these vulnerabilities; however, given current development and testing techniques, completely eliminating these vulnerabilities is not an attainable goal. Working through the attacks discussed and carefully observing the results is a big step toward shipping more securely implemented software.

Exercises

The exercises presented here are designed to help you understand how implementation attacks can be applied to your application. Professional testers can use whichever application they are currently working with.

When we teach these techniques at Florida Tech, we usually pick an application before the semester begins and then students apply the attacks to this application. Students working on their own will ideally select an application with many inputs, some of which are delivered remotely.

Once you've selected your application, perform the following exercises:

1. Write down the tasks that your application performs that require special privilege, such as changing options or writing to a file.

2. For each of the actions identified in Question 1, write down how the application checks to see who the current user is and the restrictions on the action to be performed. Some of these you may have to guess at.

3. Write down all the file types that your application reads. For each type, identify its privilege. As an example, think of a web browser that opens certain files automatically and others it asks the user if they wish to open that file.

4. Make a list of any memory-intensive tasks your application may perform on sensitive data. Ask yourself if it's necessary to store some of this information to the disk during computation.

5. Use your answers to the preceding questions to help work through the attacks in this chapter. Record your results.

PART 4

Applying the Attacks

CHAPTER 6
Planning Your Attacks

Chapter 1 introduced a fault model to guide security testing. Chapters 2 through 5 applied this model through a series of testing techniques designed to expose security vulnerabilities in software. This chapter will take security testing one step further and apply the lessons of the previous chapters to three target applications: Windows Media Player 9.0 (Windows), Mozilla Web Browser 1.2.1 (Windows), and OpenOffice.org 1.0.2 (Linux). Our targets were chosen because they have strong market presence and are fairly widely used. For each application, we will discuss in detail how each attack can be applied to that application. The attack explinations will focus on *method* and walk you through specific scenarios that can be applied. Our goal in this chapter is not to give examples of new vulnerabilities, but rather to use these applications to show how a tester who is given nothing but a binary can begin to test for security concerns.

It may be considered irresponsible for us to attempt to break the security of these products in full gory detail. Instead, for each technique we will walk through how to setup an effective security attack and the type of behavior that would be considered insecure. This will help you plan attacks against your own applications. We purposely chose diverse applications that run on the most dominant platforms, Windows and Linux. We hope that this discussion of the specific issues and approaches for each application will give you a better feel for how to apply the attacks to your own products.

To aid in this process, we have chosen applications that are freely distributable, and we have included links to each on the CD-ROM that accompanies this book and also on this book's companion Website, www.howtobreaksoftware.com/security. Install the applications. Go through the attacks on each as we explain them. Applying the attacks to these sample applications will help you get the most out of this book and hone your security-testing skills.

Some Pre-Attack Preparations

Our target applications come from both the Windows and Linux worlds. Media Player brings into play the concerns of digital property rights management and piracy of digital information. Mozilla raises the issue of protection of the client from malicious scripts and other executable content on the Web. In using OpenOffice.org, we will explore a variety of threats to the end user. Mozilla and Open Office are especially interesting subjects because not only are those applications freely available but so also is their source code.

The sections that follow will describe each of the applications. Our focus is on security-testing goals relative to those applications and which types of behavior are considered insecure. For each application, we list potential security threats. The lists are by no means exhaustive and are not intended to be the primary guide to testing. Thinking through these threats, though, will increase your sensitivity to symptoms of unsafe behavior, help you to determine the applicability of specific attacks, and allow you to more quickly diagnose security failures.

To plan your own attacks against your own applications, a first good mental exercise is to think through—relative to the target application—the three basic tenets of information security: confidentiality, integrity, and availability. Following is an outline of each:

1. **Confidentiality:** Application and user data are typically the most important resources in need of protection. Confidentiality is a wider issue, though, and also mandates that internal functionality and algorithms contained within the application are protected. Here are some questions to think through and answer:

   a. Which data and resources need to be kept confidential?

   b. Is the application itself a resource that must be kept confidential? Are piracy, uncovering algorithms, and internal implementation valid threats?

   c. Which data should the application expose, and which users should have access to that data? This brings up the important matter of digital rights management and files that the application is responsible for securing from an unauthorized or nonpaying user.

   d. What information about the system should the application not disclose?

2. **Integrity:** Integrity means that data and functionality should be modifiable only by authorized users. Under this category, we also consider the integrity of the system. This means that users should not be able to perform dangerous actions, such as executing arbitrary commands because of a buffer overflow or using escape characters to execute unauthorized commands. We must also consider the ability of an application to audit and log user actions where appropriate. Some questions to think about are:

   a. Which data should users be able to alter, and which users should be able to alter it?

   b. Which actions on the machine should be restricted?

   c. Which application files should be protected from direct user modification?

    d. What logging should be performed for user actions? How are these log files protected?

3. **Availability:** Availability means that authorized users should have appropriate and timely access to data and services. Included in this category are the notorious and highly publicized denial-of-service attacks. Think through the following questions:

    a. Which users should have access to which data and services? This is closely related to the same concern under confidentiality, but here we focus on the threat of denying an authorized user access to data or functionality.

    b. How much delay in obtaining data and services is considered acceptable?

    c. Which users have the right to deny which other users access to data and functionality?

    d. Can the application be exploited through its network interfaces to deny access to resources on the host system or be used maliciously to deny users access to other systems?

For more information and alternative approaches for developing threat models, refer to Howard and LeBlanc's *Writing Secure Code* 2nd edition (Microsoft Press 2002). Working through these questions is an important exercise. Unfortunately, many testers do not take the time to think about potential application threats before they begin to test. In functionality testing we are spoiled by spectacularly obvious failure symptoms. Displayed data may be corrupt, or the application might crash or hang; these are signs that something has gone wrong and are immediately recognizable. Symptoms of security failure are seldom as striking but are usually much more damaging.

    Thinking through potential threats before you begin testing has a twofold benefit:

1. It helps you focus each attack specifically to your product. By recognizing the threats and concerns that are relevant to *your* application, you can sharpen the attacks by customizing them to expose meaningful and security-relevant problems to the specific software you are testing. Because a security breach varies from one application to another, this can be a tremendous time saver and allow you to prioritize attacks based on the specific types of problems they are designed to uncover.

2. Understanding threats to the application and which behaviors are unsafe will make recognizing a security failure much easier.

After we have assessed the threats to an application, the next step is to start applying the attacks. For each of our target applications, we will go attack by attack, and will explain how each attack can be applied. The nature of some of our target applications means that some attacks may not be relevant. For example, no respectable bug database would ever list a vulnerability relative to reverse engineering against OpenOffice.org, an open-source product. This is where judgment and experience come into play. If the types of vulnerabilities that might be discovered by a particular attack do not represent security concerns for your application, then obviously your time would be better spent on another attack.

Included on the CD-ROM that ships with this book and this book's companion Website, www.howtobreaksoftware.com/security, are links to all three applications we will test. We strongly encourage you to spend a little time getting to know each one in order to get the most out of the attack explanations.

Target #1—Windows Media Player 9.0

Our first opponent is Windows Media Player 9.0 (WMP). WMP is designed to play a wide range of audio and visual media across multiple file formats. The player can also play streaming media—media that is read remotely and displayed in real time. The application is highly extensible through third party plug-ins and the use of CODECs[1]. WMP 9.0 can be downloaded for free from Microsoft.

Figure 6.1 shows Media Player in its default form when it is launched. Along the left hand side we see the Features taskbar, which contains but-

FIGURE 6.1 | Windows Media Player displays the Media Guide, which it loads from the Internet.

---

[1]CODEC stands for COmpressor-DECompressor. A CODEC is used by WMP to read certain file formats.

tons that link to the key Player features: Now Playing, Media Guide, Copy from CD, Media Library, Radio Tuner, Copy to CD or Device, Premium Services, and Skin Chooser. Following is a brief outline of some of Media Player's features:

1. **Media Playback of Local Files:** This is the core functionality of Media Player and arguably its most used feature. Table 6.1 shows the file formats supported by Media Player 9.0[2].

    Most file formats listed in this table represent either audio or video files. The exceptions are WMP skins, which will be discussed later.

    Something worthy of mentioning here is Windows Media Player's support for *licenses* and *licensed media files.* We quote from WMP Help: "Licensed files are digital media files that are secured with a license to prevent illegal distribution. The license specifies whether the license expires or how you can use the file." Licenses can be downloaded with media files from certain content distributors. Certain media files can be played only if their associated license has been loaded and registered

TABLE 6.1	Valid file types for Media Player
File type (format)	**File name extension**
CD audio	.cda
Intel Indeo video technology	.ivf
Audio Interchange File Format (AIFF)	.aif, .aifc, .aiff
Windows Media audio and video files	.asf, .asx, .nsc, .wax, .wm, .wma, .wmd, .wmv, .wvx, .wmp, .wmx
Windows audio and video files	.avi, .wav
Windows Media Player skins	.wmz, .wms
Moving Picture Experts Group (MPEG)	.mpeg, .mpg, .m1v, .mp2, .mpa, .mpe, .mp2v, .mpv2
Musical Instrument Digital Interface (MIDI)	.mid, .midi, .rmi
AU (UNIX)	.au, .snd
MP3	.mp3, .m3u
DVD video	.vob

---

[2]Media Player Help.

in the local Media Player. Some licensed media files also have an expiration time imposed, which effectively allows a content provider to "rent out" media to a user for a certain period of time. We'll talk about licenses more during the discussion of the Attacks.

Another interesting note is the extensibility of WMP with CODECs. When WMP attempts to play a file for which it does not have the appropriate CODEC, it attempts to connect to Microsoft's site (depending on the configured options) to download the appropriate CODEC.

2. **Streaming Media:** Windows Media Player 9.0 can also play media that is "streamed" directly from the Internet.

3. **Media Guide:** Media Guide is implemented as a miniature Web browser whose default page is WindowsMedia.com and contains active links to other pages and media. The Guide is like an electronic magazine with links to movies, music, and video on the Internet, and includes information on a broad range of topics, from international news to developments in the entertainment industry. The default view of Media Guide is shown in Figure 6.1.

4. **Copy From CD:** This feature allows the user to copy tracks from a CD and store them locally on the machine in a variety of formats.

5. **Media Library:** Media Library is a listing of media on the local machine and links to external media files. Under certain configurations, Media Player allows other local applications and Websites to access the information contained in the library listing.

6. **Radio Tuner:** Media Player allows users to receive streaming media through radio stations that are broadcast via the Web.

7. **Copying Media to CD or a Device:** Media player can be used to either transfer data to a device, such as a portable MP3 player, or send the files to a CD or other media.

8. **Skins:** The appearance of Media Player is customizable with skins when the application is in skin mode. Skins, as the name implies, change the look and feel of the application. Skins are implemented as a text file that contains characteristics of the view, a series of images, and a script file that governs behavior. Media Player comes with a selection of skins, and others can be downloaded from the Internet. Figure 6.2 shows one of these skins as applied to Media Player.

9. **Visualizations:** Visualizations are plug-ins that display splashes of color and geometric shapes that change when the music is played. There are many visualizations that come with Media Player. Users can also build their own visualizations, which are implemented as external libraries (dlls).

FIGURE 6.2	Media Player using one of its skins.

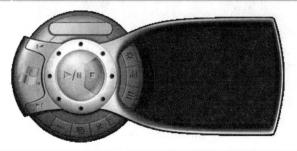

Security Threats

Windows Media Player can play both unencrypted content such as MP3, MPG, and WAV files and also media files that are encrypted, such as DVDs. The player also interacts with the network and can play streaming media directly from a remote location. Media Player also supports the use of licenses. Licenses restrict actions on certain media files and control how they can be played and distributed.

Media Player is highly extensible through the use of plug-ins for additional skins, visualizations, and CODECs. Let's consider what could go wrong with these features and what potential problems would constitute a security concern. Note that these are not vulnerabilities—rather they are possible points of attack to the application. Some of the major security threats to Media Player are:

- **Threat #1:** A user can circumvent the licensing mechanism on licensed media files. This would mean that a nonpaying user would be able to play media without a proper license—either an invalid license, a license that is valid for a different machine or user, or an expired license. For this threat, an example of a security breach would be to allow a user to play a protected media file for which they do not have a valid license.

- **Threat #2:** Creation of a malicious media file that could execute commands or cause damage to the client machine or data when played through Windows Media Player. If this can be done, then the user has the illusion of opening a "safe" file—a file which contains only data— that can be crafted to execute commands on the system.

- **Threat #3:** The system may be compromised through WMP's network interface to either read confidential data or to execute commands on the client. This is a serious concern for any network-enabled application and would certainly be considered a breach of the highest severity.

- **Threat #4:** Browse a page through Media Player's integrated Web browser in such a way that unsafe script, controls, or commands are automatically executed.

- **Threat #5:** Allows a user to play media that is theoretically restricted by parental controls. This is a lower-severity concern than the previous threats but is still something that should be investigated.

- **Threat #6:** A user is given unauthorized access to Media Library information. Windows Media Player can extend certain applications access to listings of media contained in the Media Library. A threat is that an unauthorized application or user can also access this information, compromising user privacy.

- **Threat #7:** The Media player may be made to execute arbitrary commands through either a custom visualization or skin. This is somewhat of a lesser threat, because there is no implicit trust of these files by the user. A breach here may not be considered severe unless an attacker can fake the source of these files and make them appear to come from a source trusted by the user (like Microsoft).

No list of threats involving an application of nontrivial size can be exhaustive; instead, this list merely presents some of the more obvious threats to the application, system, and user. We will refer back to it when executing our Attacks.

Attacking Windows Media Player 9.0

Dependency Attacks

Applying Attack 1: Block access to libraries

Our first step is to launch Media Player under Holodeck and look for library loads. Figure 6.3 shows the libraries that were loaded by Windows Media Player at invocation. The next step is to figure out which libraries provide which services to the application. Let's consider what type of unsafe behavior we want to expose. Recall from our explanation of this Attack (Chapter 2) that many applications rely on external libraries to provide security services to the application. You may remember that we showed how Internet Explorer's Content Advisor mechanism can be subverted by preventing a library from loading; the strategy is the same with this application. One of the most critical security features of Windows Media Player is Digital Rights Management—protecting the rights of content producers from media piracy and illegitimate use. Two specific features that we would target are the licensing feature and parental controls.

For the licensing feature, a good strategy is to monitor for library loads, either at startup or when Media Player attempts to play a licensed

FIGURE 6.3 | Holodeck monitoring Windows Media Player 9.0 for library loads.

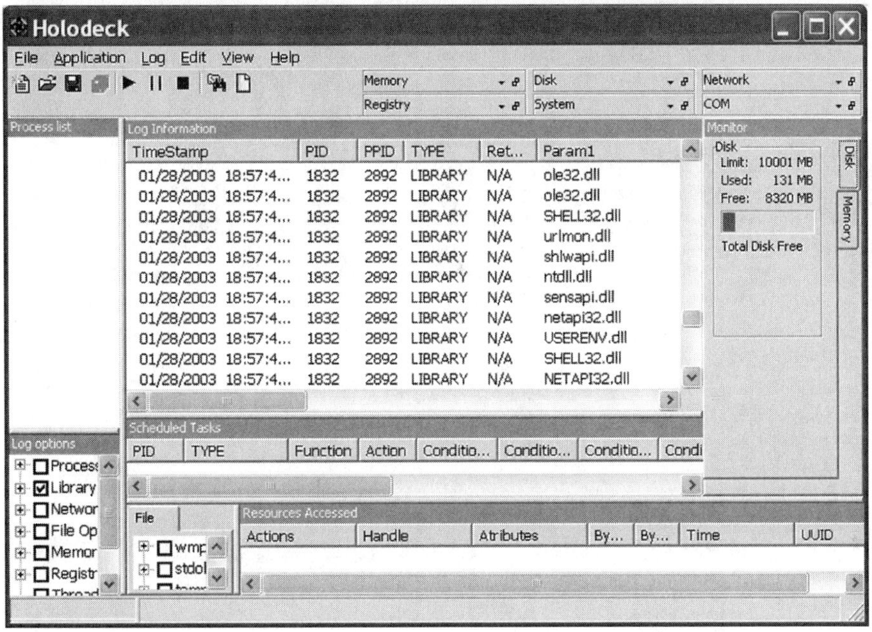

file. If you can identify a library associated with this, then a good test would be to block it and try to play a file for which you are not properly licensed. Also, internal documentation would be very helpful here in identifying library use. The same strategy applies to parental controls. A break in licensing would be a much more severe breach of security than circumventing parental controls, so this should influence the proportion of testing time spent.

Applying Attack 2: Manipulate the application's registry values

The first step is to observe Media Player's interaction with the registry at invocation. Figure 6.4 shows Holodeck monitoring Media Player's reads to the registry at startup. The biggest problem is determining which registry reads might be security related. The most severe vulnerabilities we have found with the registry involve software piracy. Because piracy of Media Player is not a concern, we must focus on the potential piracy of protected and copyrighted media. We must look at how the registry figures into Media Player's use of licenses. A good strategy is to watch a supposedly protected media file being loaded into the application and observe the registry keys that are read from or written to. For example, if the registry can be used to extend an expired license, then security is compromised.

FIGURE 6.4 Holodeck observes which keys are read by Media Player from the registry.

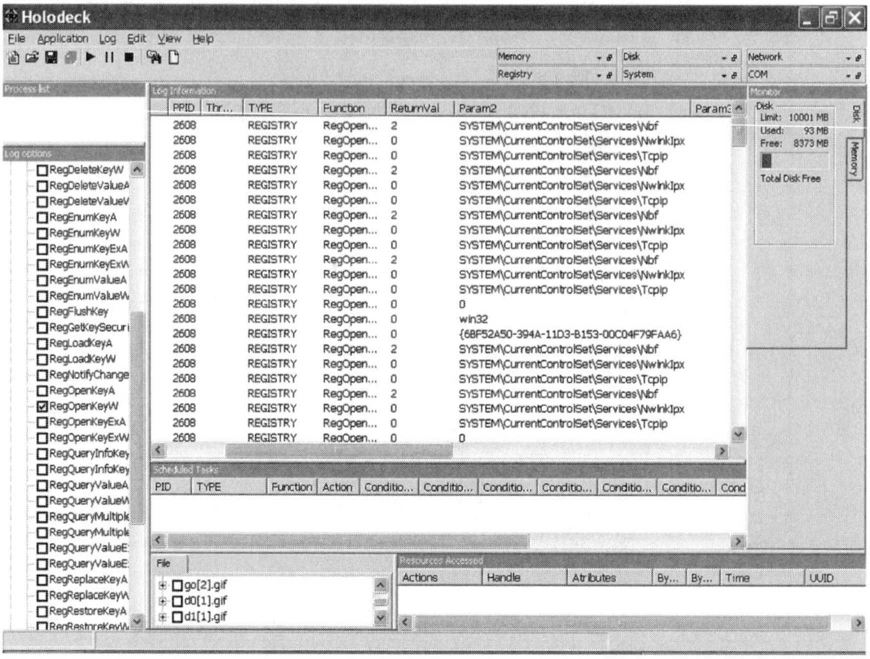

Applying Attack 3: Force the application to use corrupt files

Our goal in this attack is to create a malicious file that can be used to either crash the client or force that client to execute unintended commands. Because each of our three target applications display file contents in one form or another, this attack can be especially revealing. Our general strategy is to examine the formats of files that the viewer can read. Look for delimiters that separate data or fields that may be in the application's header. This then reduces the problem to applying string attacks (the attacks of Chapter 3) to this data. Try long values, escape characters, commands, and the like. Ideally, you should write automation code to do this for you. This can be a very simple procedure that understands a particular file format and then applies random strings of varying lengths to those fields. The automation would either create new files or corrupt existing ones, save them, open them in WMP, and check to see whether a crash has occurred.

As mentioned earlier, our first step is to find out which file types Media Player reads. These can be found in Table 6.1 at the beginning of this chapter. Our next step is to dissect these file types, looking for delimiters and fields that the application reads. The Holy Grail would be to find a buffer overflow in code that reads one of the fields in a file. If we can get this to happen, the implication is that a user who opens an assumed-to-be-innocuous media file can then have their machine exploited by commands contained in that file.

Another corruption issue on the Windows operating system is the reliance on file extensions. Users and applications often make security decisions based on file extensions. For example, a user would be more likely to download a text file than a Word document because of the risk of malicious macros in ".doc" files that is not perceived to exist in ".txt" files. The same is true of Media Player files. A user may be much more inclined to download files with an ".mp3" extension than those with some unknown extension that may have the ability to run script, change configurations, or execute other commands. Thus one fruitful avenue of file corruption is to change the extension on a file name to that of a different format—perhaps one that is assumed to be safe such as the MP3 file format. Take, for example, a recent vulnerability reported in Media Player 8[3]. Media Player 8 reads files and interprets them based on header information contained in the file itself. The critical security fallacy here is that the user makes execution decisions based on a different information source—usually the file extension—than the application does. This vulnerability means that a user could download what they perceived to be an innocuous MP3 file when they are actually downloading a file in a format that may allow executable content.

Applying Attack 4: Manipulate and replace files that the application creates, reads from, writes to, or executes

Licenses are the key focus for this attack. Licensed media is encrypted on the client and is decrypted during playback using a key contained in the license. The process of decrypting the music and playing it is seamless to the end user. In this attack, our goal is to breach security by manipulating files. Most of the license-issuing process is encrypted. The best approach, then, is to track data as it is sent to the authority that grants the license and determine where that license data is then stored persistently on the disk. If this data can be manipulated so that a license can either be extended or information can be extracted to illegally "transfer" a license from one machine to another, then security is breached.

Another approach is to observe which libraries are loaded to perform the on-the-fly decryption of the media. With a fair amount of work, an attacker may be able to replace these libraries with their own. This would allow them to decrypt media that has a valid license and then save that media in unencrypted form.

As security testers, it is critical to ensure that integrity checks are being performed on key libraries to protect against them being replaced or tampered with.

---

[3] http://online.securityfocus.com/archive/1/259028/2003-02-07/2003-02-13/2

Applying Attack 5: Force the application to operate in low memory, disk-space and network-availability conditions

Depriving almost any application of memory and disk space will cause it to fail, and Windows Media Player is no exception. The problem is finding failures—crashes or hangs—that leave the application or its data in an insecure state, which shifts our focus back to licensed media. The fatal flaw with any media-encryption scheme is that data must eventually be decrypted in order to be used. Decrypted data must reside in memory, even if only fleetingly. In some of the Attacks that follow, we will show how this can be exploited and how to test to ensure that hackers cannot access and copy this data directly. For this Attack, however, our goal is to try to force Media Player to expose unencrypted and protected data to the file system by denying the application enough memory to complete its tasks. Decryption can be a very memory-intensive process. By restricting the amount of memory available to Media Player, we can force data in memory to be "swapped" to disk. Media Player may do this automatically through the use of temporary files (a potential vulnerability that will be addressed in a future Attack), or the operating system may do it by using a memory swap file.

We can use Holodeck to restrict the memory available to Media Player while still allowing the tester access to system memory in order to observe the results. This is where Holodeck really shines. Traditional methods of memory stress testing employ applications that fill up the entire memory of the system. In these cases, not only the target application, but also testers, would have to cope with low memory resources, making most testing tools useless. However, using Holodeck, we can zero in on our testing target and still have memory available to fruitfully observe how the application responds.

Figure 6.5 shows Holodeck depriving Media Player of memory during playback. In addition, Holodeck can monitor for file writes made by the application during this process.

User-Interface Attacks

The Attacks of Chapter 3 are designed to expose vulnerabilities exploitable through the user interface. When launched, Windows Media Player executes with the same privileges as its user. This means that if we were to discover a buffer overflow or an escape sequence that allows us to execute commands through the UI, it is unlikely that we would be able to escalate our privileges on the system. Instead, we will apply the Attacks of Chapter 3 to files that WMP reads. Files read by the application that are downloaded from a remote source can be considered as surrogate access to the application by a remote user.

Users tend to download media files in formats that they are familiar with, without fear that those files could somehow compromise their machine. For this reason, it is critical to apply the following string-based user-interface attacks to media files and thus expose any latent buffer overflow or parsing vulnerabilities that may exist relative to file input.

FIGURE 6.5	Holodeck monitors for file writes as we inject the Not Enough Memory fault to deprive Media Player of system memory.

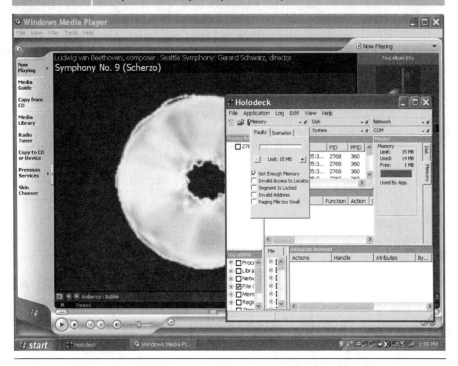

Applying Attack 6: Overflow input buffers

Buffer overflows from the file system can be found in much the same way as those exploitable from the GUI. Our first step is to look at the file formats supported by Windows Media Player. A summary of the relevant file types was presented earlier in Table 6.1.

As an example, consider Windows Media Station (".nsc") files. These are text files that reside on a server and contain configuration information about streaming media that can be viewed using Windows Media Player. If an attacker can entice a user to their Website, they can embed a Windows Media Player object in the viewed page and have it link to a ".nsc" file. The browser is then redirected to the ".nsc" file, and Media Player is launched.

The Media Player client reads data from ".nsc" files in preparation for playing the streaming-media file. A vulnerability was found in the way that Windows Media Player reads data from the IPAddress field of the ".nsc" file[4]. Apparently, data from this field is stored in a buffer of fixed size without first inspecting the data to ensure that it will fit within the confines of the space allocated. The result is a buffer-overflow vulnerability

---

[4]http://www.microsoft.com/technet/treeview/default.asp?url=/technet/security/bulletin/MS01-042.asp

that allows an attacker to craft a string to execute arbitrary commands on the client machine. Upon opening the file, WMP reads the IP address of the media server, and the malicious string overwrites portions of memory and executes commands of the attacker's choosing.

This example above illustrates that because Media Player supports a wide variety of file formats, it is a ripe target for file-based buffer over-flows. The key is to look for fields that are not limited in size by location but instead have parameter values of variable length. As an example, the CD Audio (".cda") file format is very structured. Information is identified and read by its "offset"—how many bytes it is away from the beginning of the file. This means that the length of data is limited by its location. Trying to increase the size of data in these fields would only mean overwriting additional fields.

It is more fruitful to spend time on file formats that use delimiters and previous fields to determine input length.

Applying Attack 7: Examine all common switches and options

Media Player has many options that are configurable through the UI. Consider again the threats to Media Player discussed earlier. We are concerned with license enforcement, access to the machine through the Internet by an interface opened through Media Player, and media files that can be used to execute commands. With these threats in mind, take a look at Figure 6.6, which shows the Options dialog box for Media Player 9.

FIGURE 6.6   Media Player has many options regarding network access and security that are configurable through the Options dialog box.

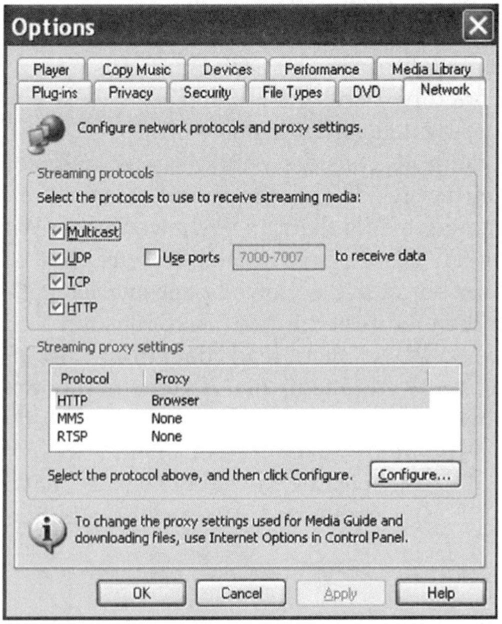

Working through options that relate to network communications, updates, and security will help you assess the potential for unsafe configurations. Finding a configuration that leaves the application exposed is a vulnerability if the user is not informed of the risks that those configurations introduce.

Applying Attack 8: Explore escape characters, character sets, and commands

File fields are susceptible to internal application-parsing vulnerabilities in the same ways that data from APIs and GUIs are. In this Attack, we will explore escape characters, character sets, and commands embedded in files read by Media Player. There are a couple of areas to look at:

- **File delimiters** are the most obvious inputs to explore in files. The file extension dictates which delimiters are valid for that file. As we saw in the application of Attack 3, files are not always parsed based on their file type or extension. It is thus important to explore a wide range of delimiters.

- **Script:** Media Player has a built-in Web browser and often displays data obtained from media files. Any time data is parsed for formatting tags and commands, there is potential to do harm. Therefore, it is critical to examine scripting and other formatting commands that influence application logic.

To illustrate, consider a vulnerability that was reported with Windows Media Player skin files. As we discussed earlier, skin files change the appearance of Windows Media Player. In previous versions of Media Player, a vulnerability was reported[5] that allowed users to embed JavaScript in skin files that could then be executed later by a hacker if the user was enticed to visit that hacker's Website. As testers, we must evaluate the risks involved in downloading files that our application reads.

Design Attacks

Applying Attack 9: Try common default and test-account names and passwords

Windows Media Player does not have any features that require authentication; therefore, this attack is not applicable.

Applying Attack 10: Use Holodeck to expose unprotected test APIs

The only test APIs that might present a threat to security are those that decrypt licensed media unsafely. Unsafe decryption would mean that the unencrypted media is exposed to the attacker, either through the file system

---

[5]http://www.microsoft.com/technet/treeview/default.asp?url=/technet/security/bulletin/MS00-090.asp

or in memory by using a test API. The strategy here is to use internal test tools that access and evaluate the playing of licensed media. Test suites that may be particularly revealing are those that are used to measure performance and playback quality. These tests are not likely to be concerned with security, and thus instrumentation may bypass some security controls on the media.

The basic approach is to watch automated test suites run and determine which libraries are loaded and which services those libraries provide.

Applying Attack 11: Connect to all ports

Open and unprotected ports are a concern with any network-enabled application, and Media Player is no exception. Our goal is to determine which ports Media Player is using to communicate with a remote source. The included port scanner is a good resource to employ here.

There are several critical times when a port scan should be run:

- During Media Player updates and CODEC downloading
- During the playback of streaming media from a remote source
- During downloading and validation of licenses
- Using the Media Guide (which browses Websites)

At each of these points, the application is communicating with a remote source, and it has to do so through a port. By identifying which nonstandard ports may be open, we can then monitor traffic passing through these ports to see whether there is a security risk. A good strategy is to check design documents, determine which data (and in what form) is passing through these channels, and verify that the actual communications are as expected.

Applying Attack 12: Fake the source of data

Windows Media Player gets data from a variety of trusted sources. One of the best examples is the way in which CODECs are loaded. These files contain information about how to play certain media files. When Windows Media Player encounters a file for which it does not have the proper CODEC, it informs the user and contacts Microsoft. By default, Windows Media Player is set to download needed CODECs automatically, as shown in Figure 6.7.

The goal behind this Attack is to impersonate a trusted source, and the obvious choice is Microsoft. This attack may involve redirecting data—at a router perhaps—to a malicious site and CODEC. It is important to determine whether Media Player takes any additional steps to verify that the data it is receiving is coming from its perceived source.

Applying Attack 13: Create loop conditions in any application that interprets script, code, or other user-supplied logic

There are two sources of input that supply logic to the application. The first are scripts that may be executable through the built-in Web browser. The second are scripts that can be embedded in files that Media Player reads.

| **FIGURE 6.7** | By default, Windows Media Player is set to automatically download needed CODECs. |

We have already seen that Media Player can execute scripts embedded in skin files. Concerns in this Attack, however, are limited to the application or client machine hanging. For a user, this may just be an annoyance rather than a serious security concern, but for system administrators, a hung application or operating environment can constitute a serious problem. Still, these concerns are not as severe as the execution of arbitrary code through a buffer overflow that may be exposed with long strings. For this reason, it may be more fruitful to spend time on attacks that may expose more serious vulnerabilities.

Applying Attack 14: Use alternate routes to accomplish the same task

The goal of this Attack is to bypass some security restriction that an application places on a task. This is a very creative process. A good starting point is to make a list of all the actions restricted by the application. For Media Player, our goals would be to determine an alternate route to access protected media. Because this is one of the few security-related actions that is restricted by WMP, it would naturally become the primary target of a hacker.

When going through the steps to download, purchase, and play a licensed media file, be mindful at each step of alternate commands you could execute to achieve the same results. Always keep the list of threats in mind, and work on alternate routes that may bypass application defenses.

Applying Attack 15: Force the system to reset values

A concern with Media Player is its default configuration and the vulnerabilities that this configuration may create on a system. As testers we must

- examine each default option,
- verify that the meaning of the option—as it is conveyed to the user—actually reflects the application's true behavior, and
- verify that these defaults do not leave the application or the system in an unsafe state.

For Media Player, our concerns regarding system integrity should guide testing. Of particular interest are ports that are opened by default, and defaults that allow the automatic downloading or execution of CODECs, media, and other data.

Implementation Attacks

Applying Attack 16: Get between time of check and time of use

Time-of-check to time-of-use issues are most often related to privilege escalation over files. Because Windows Media Player runs with the same privileges as the user, *access* to restricted files is not an issue. What's worth investigating, though, are licensed media files, and what would happen if an event or user intervened in the process of reading them, possibly circumventing expiry dates on licenses or other usage restrictions. Another interesting test case would be to investigate how Windows Media Player calculates, for time-restricted media licenses, the amount of time that has elapsed since the user contracted for the service license. By intervening in calls to either the system clock or time data from the Internet, time values can be altered, possibly subverting expired licenses.

Applying Attack 17: Create files with the same name as files protected with a higher classification

For this attack, a good starting point is to identify the files for which Media Player extends special privileges based on their name. One case that is of interest is the automatic playback of remote media files with certain extensions. Links to these files can be embedded in Web pages, and just the act of viewing certain pages can cause media to be played automatically. It is important to assess the risk of automatically executing these files and to determine which file names and extensions are extended this privilege.

Applying Attack 18: Force all error messages

Forcing error messages is almost always a useful exercise. Certainly, one feature that it is crucial to investigate is the reading and playback of licensed media. Interesting tests would involve the attempted transfer of licenses to multiple devices. There are many targets for this attack in Media Player, through both the GUI and WMP's APIs.

Applying Attack 19: Use Holodeck to look for temporary files and screen their contents for sensitive information

Temporary files can be a concern for any application that processes sensitive data. For Windows Media Player, the primary concern is that media that is restricted can be captured in unencrypted form through a temporary file. Holodeck can be used to monitor Media Player while playing protected media. After suspicious files have been identified under Holodeck, the application can be paused without giving it the time necessary to clean up these temporary files. In this state, file content can be examined.

Target #2: Mozilla 1.2.1 (Windows)

Our second adversary is the Mozilla 1.2.1 Web browser. Mozilla is an open-source application maintained by the people who collaborate through Mozilla.org. Mozilla allows users to browse the Internet and has been extended through several plug-ins. Figure 6.8 shows the Mozilla Web browser in its default view. Like many Web browsers, Mozilla supports the use of cookies, Secure Socket Layer (SSL) for secure communications, certificates, forms, and client-side scripting. Mozilla also performs standard

FIGURE 6.8 | The Mozilla Web browser.

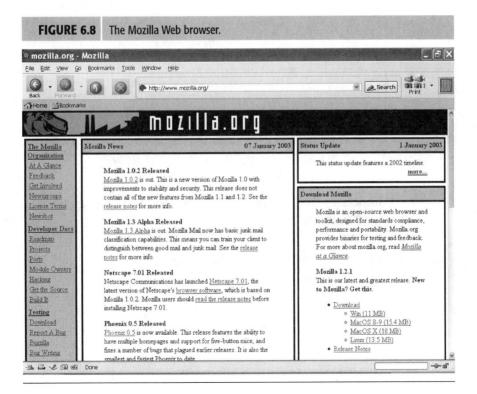

printing and saving functions, along with the option of enabling a user to apply a theme that changes the appearance of the browser.

Mozilla comes with several additional components:

- **ChatZilla**—This is an Internet Relay Chat (IRC) client that lets users send text messages to each other. The client is written in JavaScript and XUL[6] and is shown in Figure 6.9.

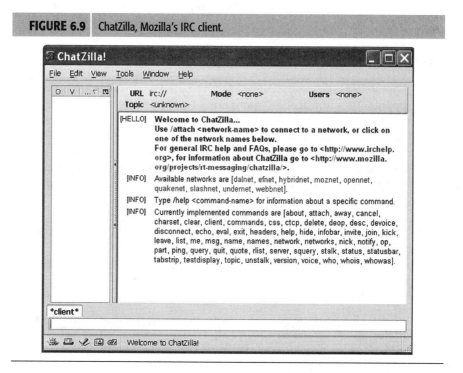

FIGURE 6.9 ChatZilla, Mozilla's IRC client.

- **Composer:** Composer is an HTML editor that allows users to create custom Web pages. It is highly extensible through the use of plug-ins (such as a spell checker). The Composer window is shown in Figure 6.10.

---

[6]XUL stands for "extensible user-interface language." It is an XML-based language for describing the contents of windows and dialogs. Where HTML describes the contents of a single document, XUL describes the contents of an entire window (which could itself contain multiple HTML documents).

FIGURE 6.10 Users can compose and edit web pages using Mozilla's Composer.

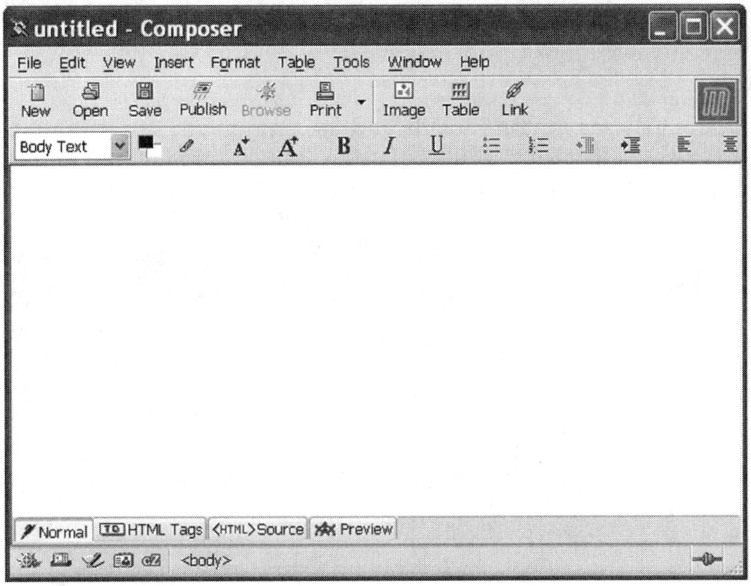

- **Mail and Newsgroups**: Mozilla also has an email and newsgroup client (shown in Figure 6.11) with which users can view, edit, and send email messages in a variety of formats (HTML, RTF, etc.). The client supports SMTP (Simple Mail Transfer Protocol), POP3 (Post Office Protocol, version 3), IMAP (Internet Message Access Protocol), and NNTP (Network News Transport Protocol). It also has the ability to send and receive attachments. Users can also manage their address books and store the names, email addresses, and other information about contacts.

Two interesting features of Mozilla from a security standpoint are its Form and Password managers:

- **Form Manager:** The following is quoted from Mozilla's user documentation: "Form Manager can save the personal data you enter into online forms, such as your name, address, phone, credit card numbers, and so on. This information is stored on your hard drive. Then, when a website presents you with a form, Form Manager can fill it in automatically." By default, Form Manager stores this data on the user's machine unencrypted. Users can set the option, however, to encrypt this data and then use what Mozilla calls a Master Password to unlock it when needed.

- **Password Manager:** This feature stores user passwords on the client machine to make logging into password-protected sites easier. Like the form data, password information, by default, is stored unencrypted on the disk. Encryption can be enabled, however, and data unlocked using a Master Password that also protects encrypted form data.

More information on Mozilla and its components can be found on www.mozilla.org or in the help documentation included with the product. Mozilla can also be downloaded for free from this Website.

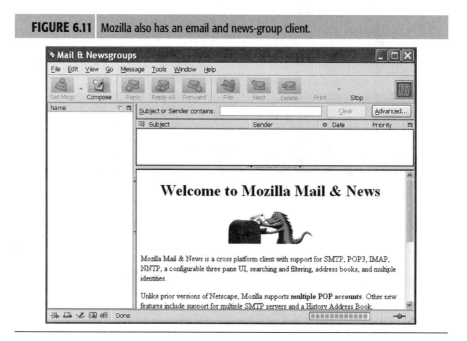

FIGURE 6.11 | Mozilla also has an email and news-group client.

Security Threats

Mozilla's main function is to allow users to view information on the Internet. As a conduit to data outside the confines of the user's machine or possibly a trusted intranet, our concern is that this conduit may be exploited maliciously. As testers, we must ensure that files, applets, scripts, and other application logic loaded by the browser cannot be used to wreak havoc on the user's machine. Also, we must consider confidential user data protected by the browser, such as cookies, form data, and passwords. Some of the more serious security threats are:

- **Threat #1:** Access to form and password data by unauthorized users. Information sent in forms and passwords is some of the most sensitive data that pass through a user's computer. We must ensure that this data is properly protected.

- **Threat #2:** Access to cookies by unauthorized Websites. Cookies often contain personal shopping habits, confidential user information, and other sensitive data that must be protected from access by unauthorized Web applications.

- **Threat #3:** Access to information about the system or its files by Web applications. An attacker can do substantial harm to a machine much more easily if they know which applications are running on a machine and what the directory structure looks like. We must ensure that access to system data through Mozilla or one of its components is protected.

- **Threat #4:** Execution of malicious logic supplied by an attacker. This is a huge threat to any network-enabled application. To protect against this threat, we must ensure that remote users cannot cause unsafe behavior on the machine by exploiting a buffer overflow or by using script code or other application logic launched by a visit to a particular Website.

Dependency Attacks

Applying Attack 1: Block access to libraries

Mozilla's structure is highly compartmentalized. Many components are implemented as separate modules that come together to create the functioning application. On first glance, security services that may be implemented by external libraries are not immediately obvious. There are, however, some potential candidates for scrutiny, such as Password Manager. Password Manager holds user passwords on the local machine. One option is for these files to be encrypted and a master password applied to unlock this data. It would be interesting to see how the initial encryption activities respond to failures in libraries and whether these failures are appropriately reported to users. Another interesting series of tests involve the loading and altering of security-relevant options that were previously set. These options may be enforced by a library or read through a library.

Holodeck can be used to observe Mozilla's library dependencies during security-relevant operations. Suspicious libraries are those with either revealing names or those that are only loaded during security-relevant tasks. In either case, Holodeck can be used to block these library loads and force error-handling routines to respond.

Applying Attack 2: Manipulate the application's registry values

The goal with Mozilla is to observe which keys may be used to store protected data or options. Of particular concern is storing private user data (perhaps from transactions or passwords) in the registry. The threat is that the user may have the illusion that certain data is protected, whereas the reality is that anyone with access to the machine could gain access to that data. Use Holodeck to monitor for registry interactions when storing a password or submitting form data.

The registry is also a place in which options might be stored. Look for options that are password protected (such as the "Use encryption when storing sensitive data" option shown in Figure 6.12) that should not be alterable by another system user. Many times, protection of these options is enforced in the GUI but can be changed without security controls through direct registry manipulation.

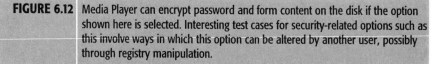

FIGURE 6.12   Media Player can encrypt password and form content on the disk if the option shown here is selected. Interesting test cases for security-related options such as this involve ways in which this option can be altered by another user, possibly through registry manipulation.

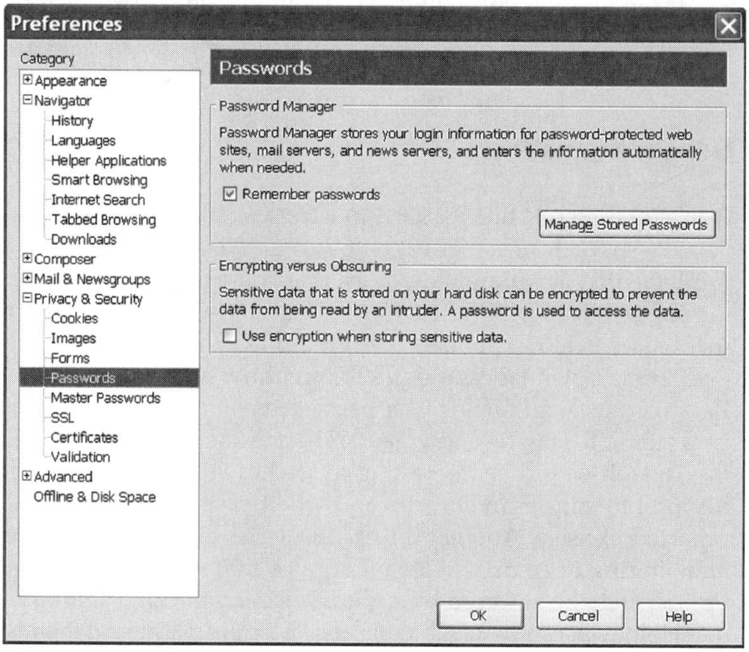

Applying Attack 3: Force the application to use corrupt files

Mozilla reads a variety of file types: HTML, pages that have dynamic content, either through script, image files or email attachments, and many others. It is too time consuming to focus on a single format and perform all possible permutations manually. The best approach is to use automation to corrupt the file formats and have them load in the browser. Obviously, intelligent automation is ideal. We want automation that recognizes tags and fields within the file and applies string attacks to these fields. For pure binary files, there is something to be said for random corruption with good automation. Remember, with random corruption of a binary, the symptom we are looking for is an application crash. Of course, a crash could have many underlying, non-security-related roots. Over the last few years, hackers have punished software makers in a very public way for buffer overflows and other vulnerabilities that allow malicious instructions to invade a system and propagate. Crashes that result from long strings or special characters have moved from being unlikely customer scenarios to high-priority potential security flaws. A crash resulting from a corrupt data file is therefore pretty likely to be noticed and fixed by developers.

Applying Attack 4: Manipulate and replace files that the application creates, reads from, writes to, or executes

There are many targets for this attack in Mozilla, such as libraries that read and store theoretically protected form and password content. The most obvious file dependencies that are fraught with risk are cookies. Sensitive information stored in cookies is certainly a security problem for a Web-enabled application. Many times, web applications rely on the fact that other Internet sites will not have access to this user information. From their perspective, they place the responsibility squarely on the shoulders of Internet browser developers to ensure that cookie data is only read by authorized Websites. From a security-testing standpoint, we must ensure that our browser enforces this separation of data.

Configuration files are another target. Like the registry, applications sometimes store user options and configurations in files that may be read at startup. We must ensure that options that are restricted from certain users cannot be altered by those users by manipulating a file. A good example is the option that is set to encrypt form and password data (shown previously in Figure 6.12). If an attacker who has access to the file system of the local machine can turn this feature off for another user, the victim may continue to have Mozilla store password data, under the assumption that that data is being encrypted.

Applying Attack 5: Force the application to operate in low memory, disk-space, and network-availability conditions

As discussed earlier, Holodeck can be used to simulate stressed memory, disk, and network conditions. For Mozilla, we must ensure that the browser still behaves securely in the absence of these resources. For example, take the act of user authentication to a remote Website. A network failure may lead the browser to write log-in information temporarily to a file while it retries the network connection. Actions such as these must be carefully scrutinized. Also, in the absence of disk space or memory, any application is almost guaranteed to fail. We must make sure that Mozilla degrades gracefully and does not dump any sensitive information to the screen or the disk as either part of an unprotected recovery file or a log file.

As we stress the application and deprive it of resources, Holodeck can still be used to monitor the file system and registry for the presence of sensitive data.

User-Interface Attacks

Applying Attack 6: Overflow input buffers

Mozilla has many sources of string input from the GUI, APIs, and the file system. Like Media Player, Mozilla runs with the same privileges as its local user. We are therefore unlikely to expose a severe vulnerability through a buffer overflow only exploitable by a local user. If a local user can execute commands through a buffer overflow in Mozilla, it is almost certain that they could execute those system commands directly, anyway. Instead, our attention must turn to data received remotely, either directly read through Mozilla or read through an API whose parameters may contain data from a remote user via another application. Perhaps the most interesting targets are files that Mozilla reads, and what might occur if we enter long strings into file fields.

Applying Attack 7: Examine all common switches and options

Like any reasonably sized application with a GUI, Mozilla is packed with user-configurable options. However, as we discussed in Chapter 3, this presents a severe scale problem. The addition of a single checkbox in configuration testing doubles the number of possible application configurations. As a simple example, consider the preferences dialog for SSL (shown

FIGURE 6.13 Mozilla has eight option checkboxes for SSL configuration. This means that if we were to run tests under all possible configurations, we would have $2^8 = 256$ possible environments to explore, just from this option panel alone.

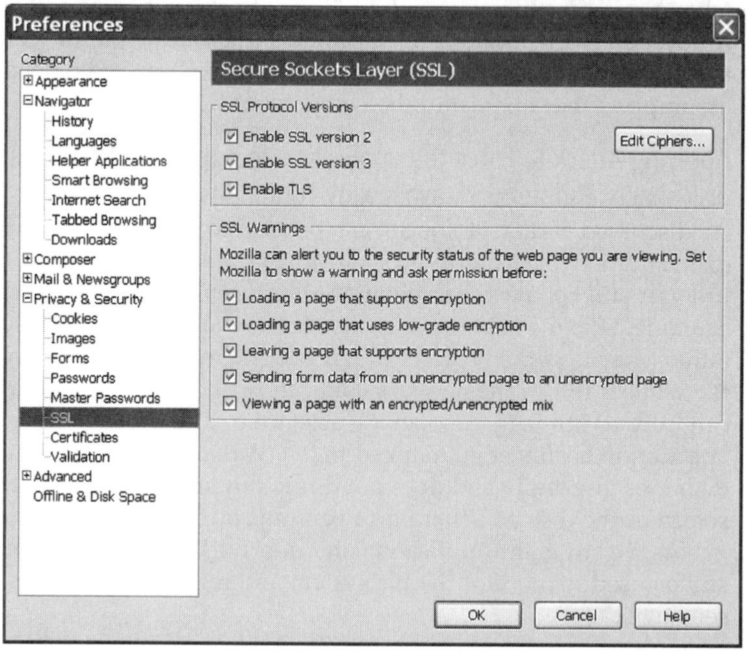

in Figure 6.13). These options alone represent 256 possible environments in which test cases can be executed.

Ideally, we would like to run a suite of test cases under each possible configuration. However, to be effective within the often highly compressed testing period, we must narrow the field of options and option combinations to thoroughly examine them. This means that rather than testing all possible configurations, we can test them in pairs or, in the case of certain options, individually. Our first focus should be on options related to network communications and those explicitly involving security. Think carefully about each option and how it may affect input filtering. Options that invoke legacy functionality can be especially revealing.

After target options have been identified, look for new inputs that may be available by enabling an option or are likely to be processed differently because a particular option is selected. A good example of this is shown in Figures 6.14 and 6.15, in which we see an input field that is only accessible if the "Limit maximum lifetime of cookies to:" checkbox is selected. Such input strings are often subjected to far less rigorous testing and may be poorly constrained internally. After one of these inputs has been identified, we can apply the other user-interface attacks presented in Chapter 3.

FIGURE 6.14 Whenever the "Limit maximum lifetime of cookies to:" checkbox is not selected, the "days" input field is disabled.

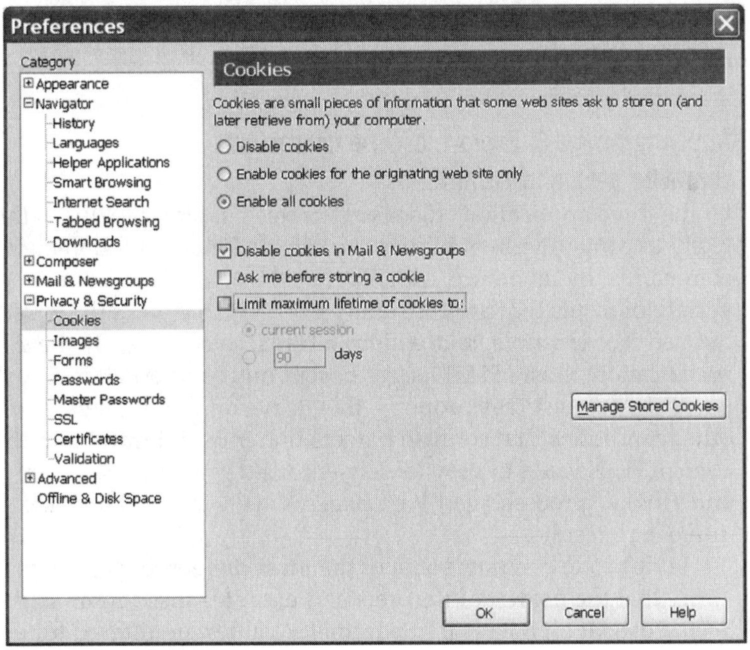

FIGURE 6.15 | If we select the checkbox, the days field is now available, and we can test it with the string Attacks of Chapter 3. Data such as this, which is likely to have been under-tested, is a fertile breeding ground for bugs.

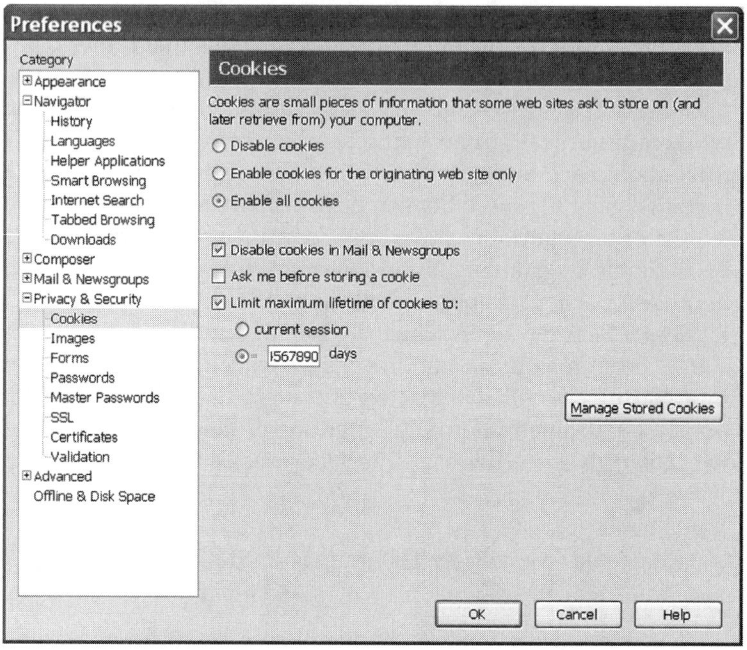

Applying Attack 8: Explore escape characters, character sets, and commands

Of the three applications discussed in this chapter, Mozilla is the most likely to contain vulnerabilities exploitable by escape characters and commands. By its nature, Mozilla must be able to process user data in a variety of forms that are constantly evolving and sometimes rather loosely defined. For example, take a simple HTML web page. By the strict HTML specification, most HTML pages hosted on the Internet are invalid. Many pages do not nest tags properly, they leave off closing tags, and create other conditions that confuse parsers that must interpret and then display content. This leads to very loosely enforced grammar rules for pages and "fuzzy" processing of Web pages, which can lead to some very interesting results.

Script code contains some of the most dangerous tags. It is critical to verify that the browser interprets and executes these commands securely. Secure execution means that parameter values are filtered for escape characters and commands that are executable, based on implementation choices. Particularly revealing inputs involve nested tags, in which commands may be treated differently if they are contained within another set of tags.

Consider a recent vulnerability reported on bugtraq[7]. The vulnerability was exploitable by inserting escape characters into a URL involving an FTP view. Scripting commands in the URL were automatically executed when the browser was redirected to the malicious URL from a hacker's site. Following is a sample exploit that creates an alert box; it could just as easily be crafted to execute malicious commands on the user's machine:

```
<a href="ftp://ftp.mozilla.org/
#%3C%2ftitle%3E%3Cscript%3Ealert(%22exploit%22);
    %3C%2fscript%3E">Exploit</a>
```

This vulnerability has since been fixed, but it serves as a good example of how escape characters can be used to execute commands.

Design Attacks

Applying Attack 9: Try common default and test-account names and passwords

As a browser, Mozilla is used to process many passwords that are used to authenticate a user on a remote machine. Mozilla has very few places in which the browser itself requires authentication to perform some task. One such place, however, is the Master Password that controls access to encrypted user data, such as Internet passwords and form data. Our goal here is to try common accounts and passwords. Table 4.1 of Chapter 4 is a good place to start. A good strategy is to look through application test scripts and harnesses that test the retrieval of protected information. These scripts may use test accounts that are hard-coded into the application.

Applying Attack 10: Use Holodeck to expose unprotected test APIs

The general strategy of this attack is to watch test automation run while logging library loads of the application with Holodeck. For Mozilla—an open-source product that relies heavily on the user community for testing—it is unlikely that testing hooks and libraries are included in the product. A more fruitful approach may then be to use functionality APIs and ensure that they are constrained with the same security controls as they would be if equivalent actions were performed through the GUI. For Mozilla, our main focus would be on APIs that retrieve password-protected user data. We will discuss this strategy further in Attack 14.

---

[7]http://www.securityfocus.com/archive/1/286150

Applying Attack 11: Connect to all ports

This is a ripe area for attack in Mozilla. Mozilla opens and exchanges data through several ports. As a Web browser, Mozilla opens ports to receive and send data to Web servers. Mozilla's IRC component ChatZilla also opens ports for communications. For this Attack, we need to ensure that data passing through an open port is appropriately filtered.

To get below the surface, we need to monitor traffic flowing through these ports. To do this justice, you may want to employ a protocol analyzer (packet sniffer) in order to be able to scrutinize data actually leaving your machine. One of the best free ones we have found is Ethereal (www.ethereal.com). With this tool, you can watch data that is being sent or received and monitor it for sensitive information.

Applying Attack 12: Fake the source of data

One feature that is common among most Web browsers is the use of cookies. Cookies are used to store Web application data and user information that is used in future Web sessions. There are many identity-impersonating tactics, which we can use to change the values of cookies directly to make a Web application believe that one user is actually a different user. These, however, are authentication problems with Web applications.

Our concern with Mozilla is to ensure that a remote user cannot access the cookie information of another Web application or domain. Cookies are created by a particular Web application and are designed to be protected (by the browser) from being read by another Web application. For example, you may login to an online banking system that stores your bank-account number in a cookie on your machine (storing sensitive information like this in a cookie is a security breach in itself, but such data is routinely kept in cookies). Now assume that you are browsing the Web and happen to end up at an attacker's Website. This site should not be able to access cookies stored by your banking application. Mozilla is supposed to check the source URL (that of the attacker) and only divulge cookie information that was set by that Web page or domain and not expose cookie data set by your bank. We must ensure that it is not possible for an attacker to fake their domain and gain access to cookies set by other Websites.

As an example, a problem was reported with Mozilla divulging cookie information by an attacker supplying an address that closely mimics a genuine address. For example, an attacker with malicious site www.hackmozilla.com could gain access to your cookies from a site like amazon.com by redirecting you to the URL using the Web address

```
http://www.hackmozilla.com%00www.amazon.com
```

Such a URL caused Mozilla to connect to www.hackmozilla.com, the hostname specified before the "%00", and divulge cookies to the server based on the entire hostname. This is an interesting exploit, because it employs both the use of escape characters (the "%00" is the URL encoded version of the NULL character, used in C to terminate strings) discussed in Chapter 3 and the idea of faking the source of data.

Using a mimicked identity to enable an attacker to read cookies is only one application of this Attack. To get the most out of this technique, you need to try to understand which features or data of your application are restricted to certain users and then try to fake the source of requests for that resource.

Applying Attack 13: Create loop conditions in any application that interprets script, code, or other user-supplied logic

Mozilla accepts user-supplied logic as one of its primary features. Every time the application "reads" a Web page that contains script code, we must ensure that that script executes securely. Secure execution of individual commands should have been guaranteed through testing the application using the previous attacks. In this Attack, however, our concern is that application logic from a remote source can cause the browser to execute seemingly innocuous commands in a long (or even infinite) loop to consume resources. Our primary assault tool for Mozilla is JavaScript. JavaScript gives a user the ability to create loops with a wide range of constructs, including:

- `for` Loops:

  `for` (*initial-expression; condition; increment-expression*)
  {*statements*}

  or

  `for` (*variable in object*)
  {*statements*}

- The `do...while` Loop

  `do`
  {*statements*}
  `while` (*condition*);

- The `while` Loop

  `while`
  {*statements*}

If, in the body of one of these loops, we can execute a command or series of commands that consumes a local resource that is not properly limited by controls in the browser, then security may be compromised. Effective commands to try are those that consume memory or disk space, such as launching a new instance of the browser (which consumes memory) or repeatedly writing new cookies in an infinite loop (which consumes hard-drive space).

Applying Attack 14: Use alternate routes to accomplish the same task

Most Windows applications have multiple routes for accomplishing the same task; this redundancy is inherited from the operating system. For Mozilla, we must first identify those tasks that require privilege and, for each of these tasks, identify the restriction mechanism we are trying to bypass. Our first target is Mozilla's restriction on password and form data from unauthorized users. The normal path to accessing this data is through the GUI, and if the user has chosen to have that data encrypted, we are prompted for a password to access the data. Some of the other routes we can attempt to use to get to this data are:

- directly from the file system
- through one of the other Mozilla components, such as Composer
- by attempting to determine which configuration files the application uses to store user information, and then altering it in a way that will force the application to expose password and form data.

The list goes on and on.

By trying these techniques, you may be able to find subversive routes to the application's protected data.

Applying Attack 15: Force the system to reset values

The concern with Mozilla is that default values and configurations can leave the application in an unprotected state. There are several defaults to look out for. First, we need to examine the options set on the application at install time to determine security-out-of-the-box. Then, in options boxes, try to delete values or leave fields blank to force the application to provide values (that we must then verify are legal and secure). As an example of out-of-the-box security, consider a vulnerability that was reported in the way that Mozilla deletes local email[8]. A user deletes email by dragging a message into the trash folder. The user can then right-click on the trash folder and Empty Trash. Messages in that folder are no longer accessible by the user and appear to have been deleted from the machine. The messages, however, still remain on the client in plaintext. They are only *flagged* as deleted. It is only when the user chooses to compact the folder that originally contained the deleted email message (such as Inbox, not the Trash folder), that the deleted messages are permanently removed.

Implementation Attacks

Applying Attack 16: Get between time of check and time of use

Mozilla is a prime target for this attack. Web browsers deal with applications (Web applications) that have a hard time maintaining state. This type of client-server relationship opens up many opportunities for a user to intervene between transactions. Observe multistep actions involving security-related tasks such as password retrieval and think of creative ways to interrupt these tasks.

Applying Attack 17: Create files with the same name as files protected with a higher classification

Mozilla reads a wide variety of file types and embedded objects. Some files are assumed to be innocuous and are thus opened automatically without

---

[8]http://lists.insecure.org/lists/vulnwatch/2003/Jan-Mar/0000.html

first alerting the user. Other files—which may have embedded code or objects—are restricted in the actions they can perform. With viewer applications such as Mozilla, we must ensure that trust extended to certain files and file types cannot be exploited by an attacker.

Applying Attack 18: Force all error messages

Trying illegal input and watching the application respond is usually a very fruitful testing exercise. When choosing input, you must consider qualities like length, input type, and boundary values. For Mozilla, this serves two purposes:

- It tests the robustness of the browser to bad data such as corrupt images, bad page-header information, and malformed formatting and script tags.
- It exposes error messages that will be returned to a user, so that they can be scrutinized to prevent the application from revealing sensitive information.

For this second goal, possibly the largest threat of exposing user or system information through errors lies in ChatZilla. Because ChatZilla communicates directly with another user, it is important to ensure that if bad data is sent to a client on Machine A from Machine B that the error returned to Machine B does not reveal sensitive information about Machine A. Another issue is error messages received when trying to connect to ports opened by these applications. With the included port scanner, you can check to see that errors are appropriate and not revealing to an attacker.

Applying Attack 19: Use Holodeck to look for temporary files and screen their contents for sensitive information

There are two things to be concerned about here:

- Mozilla exposing sensitive data it is hiding from the application user to a temporary file. Because Mozilla runs with the same privilege as its user, this is unlikely to be a severe threat.
- Mozilla writing out sensitive information belonging to its user to a temporary file. The concern is that other users of the machine or remote users may then have access to this data.

Observe Mozilla as it stores form and password information and also when it conducts transactions via the Web. If temporary files are written, you can pause the application with Holodeck and search their contents for sensitive data.

Target #3: OpenOffice.org 1.0.2 (Linux)

Despite its Web-address-sounding name, OpenOffice.org is an open-source application that offers services similar to those in Microsoft Office, including a word processor, a spreadsheet, and an application used for composing and presenting slides. We will use OpenOffice.org 1.0.2 operating on Slackware Linux 8.1. OpenOffice.org includes key desktop applications, such as a word processor, spreadsheet, presentation manager, and drawing program, with a user interface and feature set similar to other office suites. OpenOffice.org also works with a variety of file formats, including those of Microsoft Office prior to Office 2000. Figure 6.16 shows OpenOffice.org's word processor (Writer). This editor extends a wide variety of features to the user, including the ability to insert and edit pictures and spell-checking capabilities. OpenOffice.org also has editors for presentations (Impress), equations (Math), spreadsheets (Calc), pictures (Draw), and macros (Basic).

FIGURE 6.16   OpenOffice.org's word processor.

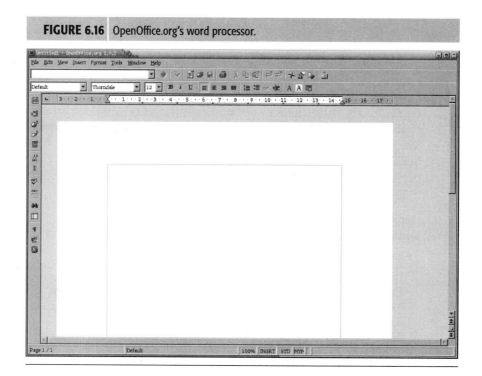

From a security vulnerability point of view, OpenOffice.org's macro feature stands out. Figure 6.17 shows OpenOffice.org's Basic editor, with which users can write and edit macros in a BASIC like syntax. The language is essentially a beefed-up scripting language and makes the OpenOffice.org GUI highly extensible.

> **FIGURE 6.17** OpenOffice.org can also run macros, and ships with a macro editor called Basic. Its macros are written in a language similar to the BASIC programming language.

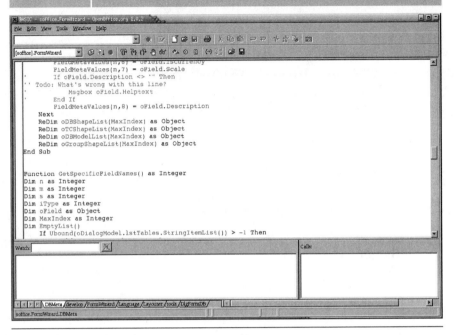

More information and documentation on OpenOffice.org can be found on its Website (you guessed it), www.openoffice.org. You can also download a free copy of OpenOffice.org from this Website.

Security Threats

The ability of OpenOffice.org to work with a wide variety of files and file types is both a blessing and a curse. This feature certainly enhances the application's usefulness, but it also introduces many potential vulnerabilities that then require checks that must be performed on the header and formatting tags of applications to validate data and ensure safe behavior. The primary threat is that a document, image, or template file can be crafted such that it forces OpenOffice.org to engage in unsafe behavior. For some document types, the risk a user takes in opening a file from an unknown individual is unavoidable and apparent. One example of these types of files is the Microsoft Word (".doc") format, which has the ability to execute macros. The real threat, however, is from file types, such as graphics files and images, that do not have this ability and are thus assumed to be safe. The danger is that data contained in these files may be able to overflow some under-allocated buffer and execute commands on the system. Some specific threats are listed below:

- **Threat #1:** A malicious file in a supposedly "safe" format can be used to execute arbitrary commands on the machine.

- **Threat #2:** Components of OpenOffice.org that connect to the Internet can create a remote channel of attack to the system.

- **Threat #3:** OpenOffice.org can be exploited to gain unauthorized access to other users' data.

- **Threat #4:** The password protection feature that OpenOffice.org offers for documents can be subverted. The threat is that a user who does not have the password to access a certain document can either read or manipulate sensitive data within that document.

- **Threat #5:** The Macro and scripting features of OpenOffice.org can be exploited to execute unauthorized commands on a user's machine.

Dependency Attacks

Applying Attack 1: Block access to libraries
OpenOffice.org has very few security services, and thus the denial of a library may cause the application to fail, but it is doubtful that this failure would impact security. One possible exception may be in the use of password-protected documents. Another interesting scenario would be if we were able to replace a library that OpenOffice.org uses with one that executes some malicious task. This could then be a threat if a victim logs into the system and runs the OpenOffice.org application, which in turn executes the exploit. This scenario is explored in Attack 4 following.

Applying Attack 2: Manipulate the application's registry values
Linux does not use a structure like the registry to hold application data. Arguably, the Linux equivalent of the registry (sort of) are various configuration files. These are files that applications use to hold application-configuration data. These are usually text files and can be edited and read by someone with the appropriate permissions. The main concern with OpenOffice.org is that these files are not used to store sensitive user information in plaintext.

Applying Attack 3: Force the application to use corrupt files
For security, we must test that OpenOffice.org responds appropriately when it receives a corrupt file from a remote user. In particular, we want to ensure that a file that is downloaded by a user running OpenOffice.org cannot be corrupted in such a way as to force the application or system to execute arbitrary commands or corrupt other data. Testing using this attack would ideally involve intelligent automation that is aware of the

file formats read by OpenOffice.org and could be used to insert strings, escape characters, and reserved words into file fields. The next step would be to look for application crashes; these may indicate a buffer overflow.

Applying Attack 4: Manipulate and replace files that the application creates, reads from, writes to, or executes

One of the biggest concern with OpenOffice.org is that the application may be forced to create files that overwrite protected system or user files. One such attack vector is through the popular Linux and UNIX hard link. There is also the possibility that if a user has access to libraries and other dependencies, these could be replaced by malicious files that would execute commands of an attacker's choosing when the victim launches OpenOffice.org.

A good example was reported with Star Office, an office application that shares most of the same code base as OpenOffice.org but is sold commercially through Sun Microsystems. The vulnerability exists in a version of Star Office that predates the OpenOffice.org movement.

This vulnerability takes advantage of the fact that the application shares access to a temporary directory with other Star Office users[9]. The application saves temporary data in the `/tmp/soffice.tmp` directory, which it creates with world-writeable permissions (read/write for any user). The problem is compounded by the fact that the application appears to change the permissions on this folder after it accesses it to *ensure* that it is world writeable. Imagine a user A who does not have access to a file owned by user B. Because user A can overwrite the `/tmp/soffice.tmp` directory, he or she can also replace it with a link to another directory or file owned by user B. The next time B launches Star Office, it follows the symlink from the directory `/tmp/soffice.tmp` (created by user A) to the protected file of user B. Star Office then sets permissions on user B's file such that any user can read or write to it. This is a severe vulnerability, because user A could potentially access a shell start-up file (e.g., `~/.profile, ~/.bashrc, ~/.cshrc,` etc.) that could then be modified to execute commands of A's choosing the next time user B logs in.

Applying Attack 5: Force the application to operate in low memory, disk-space, and network-availability conditions

Because Holodeck does not operate on Linux, you may need to employ more traditional methods of fault injection. There are many stress tools available that simulate user activity on the system. However, fault injection of the application's environment is usually done to force the application to invoke error-handling routines that expose sensitive data. OpenOffice.org protects little data from its local user, though, and thus this attack is unlikely to expose any severe security-related problems.

---

[9] http://www.securityfocus.com/archive/1/163948

User-Interface Attacks

Applying Attack 6: Overflow input buffers

Long strings in fields are a good way to expose buffer overflows through the GUI. Because the application runs with the same privilege as its user, this is not particularly interesting from a security point of view. Instead, the preferred approach would be to corrupt files that the application reads. These files can be viewed as surrogate access to the machine by a remote user. Because OpenOffice.org reads files from Microsoft's Office, a good approach would be to search bug databases such as bugtraq (available at www.securityfocus.com) for file formats that attackers have been able to exploit in that product. Once you have some candidate files, the best approach is to write intelligent automation that is aware of the target file structure and can try long strings in fields, open the affected files with OpenOffice.org, and watch for a crash.

Applying Attack 7: Examine all common switches and options

The most critical options that should be investigated with OpenOffice.org are those related to the execution of macros in documents. Tests should be run under the available macro configurations to ensure that option descriptions provided to the user accurately reflect the application's behavior. Pay special attention to default options and ensure that the application errs on the side of security.

Applying Attack 8: Explore escape characters, character sets, and commands

Like the buffer-overflow attacks, escape characters and commands that are executed by the application are only interesting if they come from a remote user. Thus our attention turns again to file corruption in which automation inserts various escape sequences and reserved words into files read by OpenOffice.org and observes the results. Unlike long string attacks (where the application is likely to crash if a vulnerability is uncovered), files sprinkled with escape sequences and commands may expose insecurities in a more subtle fashion. You need to monitor for odd error messages that may indicate that a script or command was about to be executed but that there was a syntax problem.

Design Attacks

Applying Attack 9: Try common default and test account names and passwords

The only feature that OpenOffice.org has that uses passwords is the protection of items and settings within individual documents. This Attack involves attempting to open protected documents. Keep in mind that the goal is not to crack the password of an individual document. Instead, we want to expose any undocumented accounts in the application that may be used across all or a set of documents. Again, looking at test scripts and harnesses is a good place to start. Isolating the routines that unlock a document and reviewing the source code for these routines may also prove fruitful.

Applying Attack 10: Use Holodeck to expose unprotected test APIs

As an open-source application, OpenOffice.org is unlikely to contain test instrumentation that is exploitable by the user. With this in mind, resources should instead focus on functionality APIs that access OpenOffice.org's only explicitly protected resource: documents that are locked with a password.

Applying Attack 11: Connect to all ports

Like the other two applications tested, this Attack involves scanning the machine for ports opened by the application. The Linux machine running OpenOffice.org can be scanned from a Windows machine with the port scanner included on the CD-ROM. There are also many freely available port scanners that run on the Linux platform. One of the best we have come across is NMAP (www.insecure.org/nmap/). This tool is freely available on multiple platforms and has the ability to monitor data entering and leaving the system.

Applying Attack 12: Fake the source of data

One specific concern is that document types can be mimicked. Because Linux does not enforce the use of extensions to identify document types, an attacker could possibly coax a user into opening a file that has the ability to execute scripts and macros. Test scenarios involve altering document fields and formats to determine how the application validates document types before they are granted the right to execute scripts or macros.

Applying Attack 13: Create loop conditions in any application that interprets script, code, or other user-supplied logic

OpenOffice.org can run macros. With this Attack, we must verify that a malicious file with embedded macros that execute "safe" functions cannot force the application to consume system resources maliciously. Also important to check are any scripts or recursive references within a document.

Applying Attack 14: Use alternate routes to accomplish the same task

This Attack is usually used to circumvent some control on actions or data restricted from the user. Like all Linux applications, OpenOffice.org relies on the operating system to enforce the permissions assigned to files. With regard to the application itself, the vulnerabilities that may be exposed through this attack relate to circumventing security-related controls around password-protected documents. The key is to think through access routes to password protected files and verify that each enforces the restrictions set by a user on a document.

Applying Attack 15: Force the system to reset values

Default values are always a security concern. Our first mission should be to ensure that the application is in a secure state out of the box. This means verifying that options default to those that protect user data and the integrity of the system. Also, check the documents that OpenOffce.org produces to ensure that permissions are set correctly. It is also important to verify that documentation accurately reflects the application's default options.

Implementation Attacks

Applying Attack 16: Get between time of check and time of use

Finding discrepancies between when security is checked around a piece of code or data and when privileges are used requires creativity. Look for actions involving multiple steps. One route of attack may be opening a password-protected document and then changing the file so that it references some other protected file with a different password. Here we bait the application with a document that has been legitimately unlocked and then replace it with a protected document. Also carry out this attack using hard links to sensitive Linux or UNIX system files.

Applying Attack 17: Create files with the same name as files protected with a higher classification

Applying this Attack involves learning the documents to which the application extends special privilege, such as those that execute script or macro commands. The best approach for OpenOffice.org is to enumerate these file types and formats and then construct test files that take advantage of application assumptions as to file content. Especially ripe test areas are non-native file formats that the application supports, such as Microsoft Word documents. The versatility of Word documents to embed objects, script, and macros makes the developers' task to ensure secure interpretation of document components difficult. It is very easy for cases to get missed or for what may appear to be a string of seemingly innocuous actions to create unsafe conditions.

Applying Attack 18: Force all error messages

Forcing error messages in non-security-related features within the GUI is a useful exercise for testing the application's robustness to illegal input. For security, it is essential to force error messages in any inputs that originate from a remote user. Because OpenOffice.org does not accept any remote input directly (most of its interactions with the network are through other applications), we must turn to file-related error messages. Because files act as surrogate access to the application, we must assure that invalid inputs from files are appropriately and securely handled by the application.

Applying Attack 19: Use Holodeck to look for temporary files and screen their contents for sensitive information

The purpose of this Attack is to uncover temporary files that the application reads that might expose sensitive application or user data. In examining the threats, let's consider the temporary file vulnerabilities that may exist:

- OpenOffice.org may create a temporary file that exposes content to an unauthorized user. With regard to this concern, we must check that all temporary files that contain user data have the correct permissions set and are destroyed appropriately. Another thing to consider is password-protected files. For these documents, we must ensure that no temporary files exist that contain document contents.

- OpenOffice.org may create a temporary file that can be altered by an unauthorized user to either execute unauthorized commands or alter another user's data. In the application of an earlier Attack, we saw a vulnerability in OpenOffice.org's commercial incarnation, Star Office, in which the creation of a temporary file opens the application to attack. For OpenOffice.org, we must inspect file permissions on temporary files to ensure that another user's document content cannot be modified or that scripts or macro commands cannot be inserted into another user's document.

Summary

In this chapter we applied the Attacks of Chapters 2 through 5 to three applications: Windows Media Player 9.0, Mozilla 1.2.1, and OpenOffice.org 1.0.2. For each Attack description, we focused on methods for exposing vulnerabilities rather than on specific test cases. To get the most out of this book, we strongly encourage you to install at least one of these applications and work through the Attacks.

Exercises

The exercises presented here are designed to help you get a feel for applying the attacks in this book to real applications. Pick one of the three applications studied in this chapter and perform the following exercises:

1. Install the target application and get to know its features.
2. Look through the threat list, and write down two additional threats for the application you selected.

3. For the application you chose, go to a public vulnerability database—such as bugtraq (at www.securityfocus.com)—and read through at least five actual security bugs reported against that application.

4. Conceptualize and describe one potential vulnerability that might be exposed with each Attack. For that vulnerability, write down a test case that you might try in order to expose that vulnerability.

5. Apply each of the Attacks to the application you selected.

6. Pick another application, either one that you are currently testing or an application that you may have used in the past. For this application, list the potential threats to the application.

PART 5

Conclusion

CHAPTER 7
Some Parting Advice

01100101011011000110001 100

How Secure is Secure?

Testing is a frustrating discipline. No matter how hard you work on testing a product, in all likelihood, you will find only a subset of the bugs. There are simply so many inputs and input combinations that it is unlikely you will ever be able to apply them all. Add to this that there are so many places for bugs to hide inside an application, and your task looks pretty hopeless.

It is *theoretically* possible to find every bug in an application, but even if you did, there'd be no way to prove it, so you'd still be left in doubt. Thus what you hope for is two-fold: (1) every time you test a new application, you do better than you did the previous time, and (2) you did a thorough enough job at finding all the fairly-easy-to-find vulnerabilities so that any left in the product are so time consuming to discover, that the hackers give up to target easier prey (a competitor, perhaps).

The focus for security testers must be constant improvement. This means paying attention to what you are doing and how you are doing it and ensuring that you understand what you did wrong so that it never happens again. This chapter contains some advice that may help.

Mining for Gold in Bug Databases

Developers, whether they work for your company or in a totally unrelated product area, tend to make a set of common mistakes. If we understand and focus on these mistakes, then we can design more effective testing techniques.

Understanding common design and implementation mistakes is hard work, because the mistakes made five years ago may now be moot. As technology changes, development tools change too, and we have to keep up. A practice we have found helpful is to ensure constant focus on security bugs, whether they are in your product, a competitor's product, or in a completely unrelated application. Bugs are very important because they tell us where we are going wrong. Focusing on these mistakes gives us an incredible advantage in designing test techniques that expose faulty behavior.

Public security vulnerability databases like bugtraq (available from www.securityfocus.com), CERT (www.cert.org), and others are packed with insights to help you test your own products. Because these resources publish bugs that are in released products, they tell us where our own methodologies are failing. A very useful practice is to monitor these bug reports and ask yourself the following three questions:

1. What underlying software fault caused the vulnerability? Put yourself in the developer's shoes, and try to reason about the code defect that led to the vulnerability. The more we understand how these bugs are created, the better chance we'll have of identifying their symptoms as we are testing.

2. What failure symptoms of the executing application would alert us to the presence of the fault? Obviously, because we are studying released vulnerabilities, some testers somewhere missed the bug. Either they failed to supply the right inputs to force the buggy code to execute, or it executed, and they missed it. If a bug executes, and no one is around to see it, it is still a bug. We need to train ourselves to be better at recognizing buggy behavior when we see it.

3. Would any testing technique we use have found this bug? Testers should find out which techniques in their arsenal will work best against the types of bugs that their product may contain. If no existing technique would have found the bug, then we have an even bigger problem.

As testers, we must learn from bugs. Whether they belong to our product or the products of another company, bugs are our best evidence about what we are doing wrong. We must pay attention to these mistakes and be constantly vigilant for opportunities to improve our own testing processes and tools.

Testers Are Not Librarians!

So often we have seen so-called "penetration tests" that basically correlate to a few hundred automated scripts that represent known exploits. The concept in use in this situation is that we know these exploits have worked in the past, and we want to see whether they will work on the newest product. We liken this to librarians testing software. Any time a new project comes around, we simply check our tests out of the library, execute them, and hope for the best.

The problem with our argument here is that this strategy actually works! Many security-testing vendors have built businesses on this model because of the reasons we talked about in the previous sections: developers tend to make the same mistakes over and over again. Add to this the other piece of the equation, that current software is really buggy, and you have a winning test strategy.

But this will not remain the case for long. Anyone can build and maintain an exploit library, and the competition in the security testing outsource arena is stiff with competitors. Having the best library will only be a distinguishing factor for bugs that constitute, essentially, the low-hanging fruit—that is, the easy-to-find bugs. We predict that the low-hanging fruit will mostly be picked in the very near term. When this happens, security testers will be in a race with hackers to see who can understand the next level of vulnerabilities.

We need to beat the hackers in this race. Don't fall into the librarian mentality and lose sight of the future.

Postmortems

Security testing is complicated. Testers always need to be on the alert for new attack possibilities. However, during a ship cycle, testers have many distractions that may prevent a serious focus on tactics and how to improve their effectiveness. They have bug reports to write, war meetings to attend, and so forth. Thus when a project is over and all these pressures have been alleviated by a hopefully successful release, it is time to sit back and think. This is called the postmortem examination.

Postmortems should be done immediately following release and then again when field data begins to come in. The main purpose of a postmortem immediately following release is to understand what did and did not work during the project. Take a good look at which attacks found a lot of bugs and which ones didn't. We need to determine what is working for us, what isn't working for us, and why.

We like to look at bugs from both the testing perspective and the product perspective. From the testing perspective, we want to correlate the bugs we found with the techniques that found them. This will help us understand and prioritize additional or future testing that we may need to do. Some attacks simply don't apply to some types of software, and if we are wasting our time applying these attacks, then we could use that time more wisely. Some attacks may also have been applied incorrectly, and a thoughtful postmortem may help identify whether such issues are present.

From the product perspective, we want to understand which parts of the application were most buggy and try to determine whether there was good coverage of the features that revealed the fewest defects. Did we miss anything? Are there some bugs found in one feature that may exist in a similar feature elsewhere in the product? Are some features of the application more suitable to certain attacks?

A Final Thought

You will never find every security bug in your product. Software is simply too complex, and the ever-growing feature set of modern applications has far outpaced organizational tools to manage their complexity. The result: incomplete requirements, error-prone implementation, and ultimately, bugs. Software testers are the last line of defense for an application before it gets released. We must verify that application developers have done their job and that the design and its implementation have created a functional and secure product.

As software continues to evolve, so must testing techniques that expose potential vulnerabilities. As new technologies emerge, so do new threats that must be assessed. The attacks in this book will, we hope, inspire security testers to look beyond old exploits and think clearly about security flaws and the techniques that are best at isolating them. Always keep in mind the threats to your application and its users, and use them to guide your testing.

Happy hunting!

APPENDIX A
Using Holodeck

0110010110110110001 100

Using Holodeck

The side-effect functionality that is usually responsible for insecure behavior is not in plain view during testing. A temporary file or registry write that would go unnoticed during functional testing could represent a security vulnerability of the highest severity. The truth is that it's likely that most insecure, post-release behavior like this probably occurred during pre-release testing but just wasn't noticed. To be effective as security testers, we need tools to help bring this hidden functionality to the surface. Our answer in part to this problem is a tool called Holodeck.

Holodeck has the ability to monitor interactions between an application and its environment. It traps system calls and lifts the curtain to bring them in plain view of the tester. We borrowed the name for this tool from the popular science-fiction program "Star Trek." There, the holodeck is a room that simulates the look, sound, feel, smell, and taste, of any place imaginable, completely indistinguishable from reality. Although such technology is clearly fictional (at least in the near future), it does paint a pretty accurate picture of the power our Holodeck brings to software. Our tool simulates an application's environment, allowing fine-grain control of the responses from the OS to the application under test. Consider the simple scenario of an application creating a text file. One of the system calls that must be made is to the function CreateFile. There are many reasons why this call could fail (a write-protected disk, for example). Without Holodeck, testing an application for these types of failures would require actually creating the hostile condition, such as manually filling up the hard drive or attempting to corrupt a file to cause a CRC (Cyclical Redundancy Check) error. Some of these conditions that are possible in the real world are just too cost prohibitive to create in the test lab. Holodeck, however, can simulate these failures. The following discussion outlines the features of Holodeck.

Launching Your Application Under Holodeck

You have two options for attaching Holodeck to your application:

The first option lets you launch your application from within Holodeck. Figure A.1 shows Holodeck being launched. You can then find your application's executable and have Holodeck launch the application.

| FIGURE A.1 | You first choose an application to launch under Holodeck. |

A second option for launching your application is to attach Holodeck to an already running process. Figure A.2 shows the process view of Holodeck in which a user can select an already running process to attach to.

After the target application has been selected, you are prompted with an option menu that contains configuration and logging options for your Holodeck session. These options are shown in Figure A.3.

One option that bears singling out is Predefine Tasks When Creating. This option allows testers to search for specific system calls based on parameter values and inject error codes into their return values. If this option is selected, Holodeck presents a list of system calls that can be intercepted (Figure A.4). After a system call has been selected, it can be monitored or failed, based on parameter values, as shown in Figure A.5. For a specific scenario of system calls being failed, see Attack 1 in Chapter 2. There we show system calls to load the msrating.dll library being denied. We strongly encourage you to try to reproduce the bug shown in that attack with Holodeck. This will give you a feel for how this feature works.

FIGURE A.2 Holodeck can also attach to a running application.

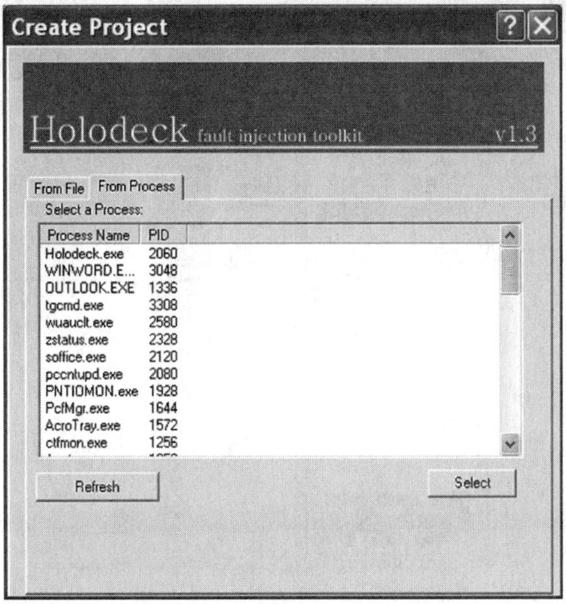

FIGURE A.3 Holodeck has a wide variety of logging options that can be set at startup.

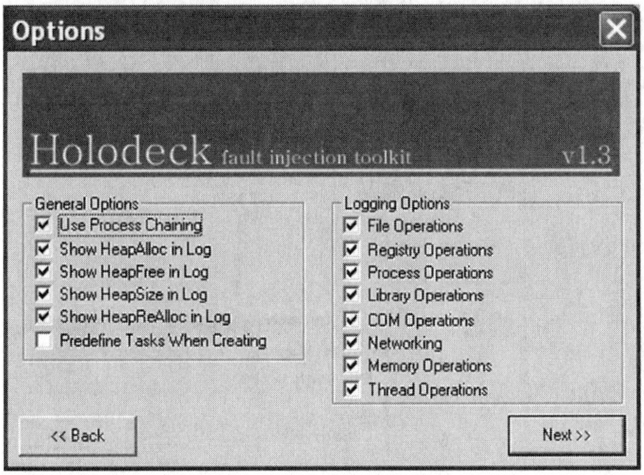

FIGURE A.4 Holodeck can be used to fail certain system calls that access application dependencies.

FIGURE A.5 After you've selected a system call to intercept, you can selectively fail these calls based on parameter values.

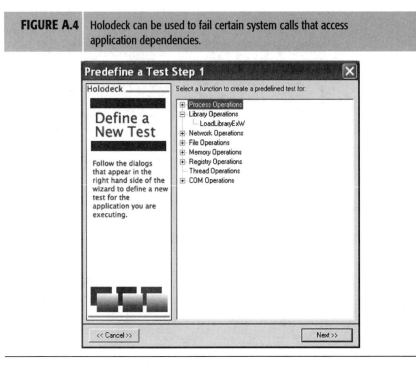

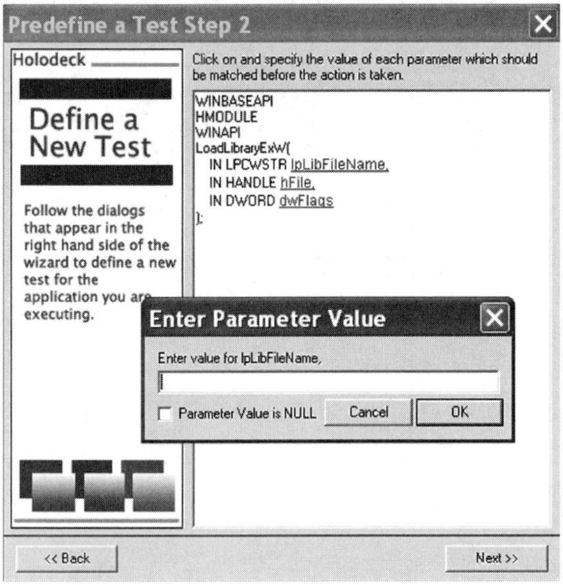

Inserting Environmental Faults

The **Network, Disk, Registry, System, COM,** and **Memory** panels constitute the fault-injection bands. Each of these bands supports certain common functionality. Figure A.6 shows an expanded view of the three most common classes of environmental faults.

FIGURE A.6 Holodeck can be used to inject a broad range of environmental faults.

Holodeck

File Application Log Edit View Help

Process list

Log Information

TimeStamp
02/24/2003 23:58:4...
02/24/2003 23:58:4...
02/24/2003 23:58:4...
02/24/2003 23:59:4...

Scheduled Tasks

PID   TYPE   F

Log options
☑ Process Operati
☑ Library Operatio
☑ Network Operat
☑ File Operations
☑ Memory Operati
☑ Registry Operati
☑ Thread Operatio

Memory

Faults | Scenarios

Limit: 1024 MB
☐ Not Enough Memory
☐ Invalid Access to Locatio
☐ Segment Is Locked
☐ Invalid Address
☐ Paging File too Small

File |

Resources Accessed

Actions   Handle

Disk

Faults | Scenarios

Limit: 10001 MB
File
☐ Not found
☐ Cannot be opened
☐ Access denied
☐ Write Protected
☐ CRC Data Error
☐ Drive cannot seek disk
☐ In Use
☐ File Portion Locked
☐ Disk Full
☐ Already Exists
☐ Cannot be Created
☐ Name too Long
☐ Read Only
☐ Path not Found
Directory
☐ Cannot be Removed
☐ Path Invalid
☐ Directory Not Empty
☐ Corrupt Structure(s)

Network

Faults | Scenarios

☐ Disconnect
☐ Network not installed
☐ Wrong Winsock version
☐ Winsock task limit reache
☐ No ports available
☐ Network is down

By... | Time

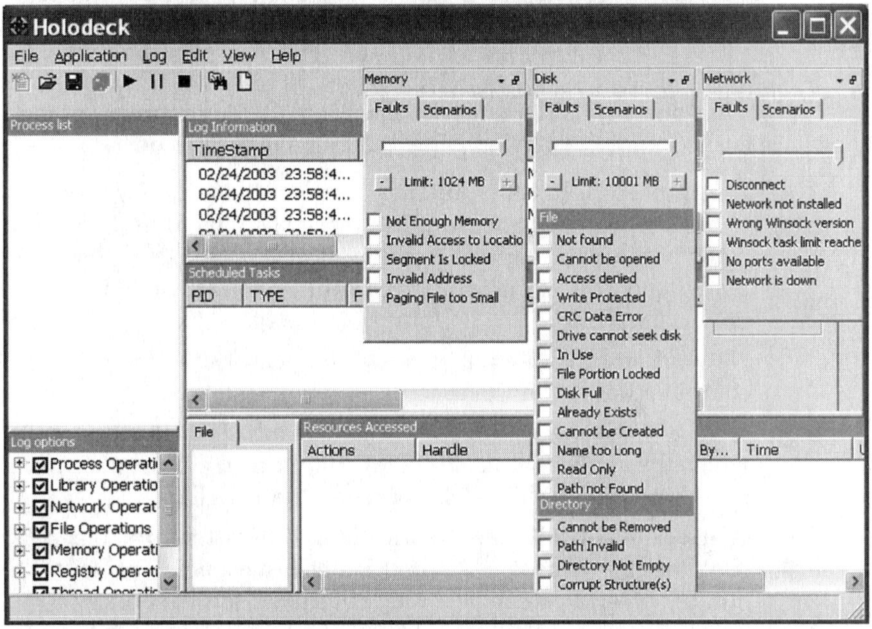

These controls allow you to inject specific faults into the environment of the application under test. We will now describe the three most commonly used of these panels and some specific faults that can be applied in each.

Network Faults

The network band allows you to simulate the following conditions.

Scenarios

The default scenario set for the application under test in the network band is Manual Control, which enables the manual control slider to control the amount of bandwidth available to the application under test. The manual control slider is set to the 100% mark by default. When the slider control is at 100%, Holodeck does not intervene in packet transmissions on the network port used by the application under test. Sliding the bar to the left allows Holodeck to simulate a network slowdown condition by delaying packet transmission.

Holodeck simulates three other scenarios that duplicate the behavior of real network conditions that can occur in practice. For example, computer networks tend to gradually slow down as new users log on and initiate network traffic. The Network Busy scenario in Holodeck simulates network slow-down behavior by presenting the application under test with a slower and slower network as you continue to test the application. The Network Problems scenario simulates a network fault pattern characterized by bursts of traffic and periods of full bandwidth. The Random Network Errors scenario randomly injects any one of the various faults described in the following list.

Network Faults

Network-oriented faults can be injected into the environment of the application under test by enabling the following check boxes:

- **Disconnect.** Holodeck simulates the network becoming unavailable to the application under test. In a real environment, the network could become unavailable to an application because of, among many other causes, an unplugged cable, software disconnection, or downed servers.

- **Network not Installed.** Holodeck simulates a situation in which the computer has no ISP or network software installed.

- **Wrong Winsock version.** Injecting this fault simulates a condition in which the application under test is running on a computer that has older versions of Microsoft's Winsock API installed.

- **Winsock task limit reached.** This fault causes a failure to be raised that simulates the Winsock API reaching its full capacity in terms of the number of applications that have requested socket services.

- **No Ports Available.** Selecting this fault allows you to simulate a situation in which all available ports on a computer are busy, down, or otherwise unavailable.

- **Network is down.** Holodeck allows you to simulate the problem of an out-of-service ISP, disabled router, or any other of the many reasons that a network could be down.

Disk

The Disk band represents failure of the file system.

Scenarios

The default scenario set for the application under test in the disk storage band is Manual Control, allowing you to use the manual control slider bar to control the amount of disk space made available to the application under test. When the slider control is at the 100% default mark, Holodeck will not intervene in file interactions of the application under test. Sliding the bar to the left allows Holodeck to restrict the amount of disk space accessible to the application under test.

Thus a smaller hard drive can easily be simulated by setting the slider control to the desired level. Holodeck will fail file-write operations when the application has used all available space. The Disk Space Fluctuating scenario causes a range of disk storage to be available to the application under test, from lots of space to very little space, on a random basis. Various File Errors randomly injects any of the various faults described in the following discussion when the application under test makes use of the file system. Random Directory Errors randomly injects some of the directory faults available.

Disk Faults

In the disk-storage band, faults can be injected into the application's environment by selecting any of the following check boxes:

- **Insufficient disk space.** When this fault is selected, Holodeck returns errors to the application under test indicating that file writes attempted by the application did not succeed, because the computer did not have enough free disk space to accommodate the write operations.

- **CRC errors.** Holodeck simulates file corruption to the application under test by returning an erroneous condition stating that the cyclical redundancy check has failed on either read or write file operations attempted by the application.

- **Too many files open.** This fault causes the file requests of the application under test to fail and an error to be returned indicating that the system has too many files open.

- **Write-protected disk.** Injecting this fault causes Holodeck to inform the application under test that the media (removable media like floppy disks, ZIP disks, etc.) is write protected.

- **No disk in drive.** This fault is another failure related to removable media issues that Holodeck simulates, indicating that there is no disk in the drive.

Memory

The Memory band represents failure of the kernel.

Scenarios

The default scenario set for the application under test in the memory band is Manual Control, allowing you to use the manual control slider bar to control the amount of memory available to the application under test. When the slider control is at the 100% default mark, Holodeck will not intervene in memory allocation of the application under test. Sliding the bar to the left allows Holodeck to restrict the amount of memory available to the application under test. Thus when the application requests more memory than the slider bar indicates, memory calls will fail.

The Varying Memory scenario simulates interoperability problems on a system in which any number of applications may contend for memory resources. Thus memory may be plentiful one moment (when none of the applications need any memory) and scarce the next moment (when several applications make memory requests at about the same time).

Memory Faults

In the memory band, faults can be injected in the application under test by selecting any of the following check boxes:

- **Insufficient memory.** Selecting this fault causes Holodeck to return errors to the application when it makes memory-allocation calls, indicating that there isn't enough memory available to fulfill the request.

- **Fail to allocate.** This fault causes the application under test to generate an error that can occur when memory is sufficiently fragmented or the computer is overly stressed.

- **Lock memory.** This fault simulates the failure of APIs intended to lock memory for the sole use of the application.

Monitoring the Application

We can monitor an application using Holodeck and watch its interactions with the environment. Application logs can be filtered using a panel on the bottom left-hand corner of Holodeck, as shown in Figure A.6. This allows testers to focus only on certain application behaviors at any single point. One useful feature of Holodeck is its ability to pause the application under test. By pausing the application, we can filter application logs and perform a detailed inspection of the application's behavior.

More information on Holodeck can be found on this book's companion web site: www.howtobreaksoftware.com\security.

APPENDIX B
Software's Invisible Users

01100101101100011100

Abstract: Developers and testers alike are comfortable with the notion of the human user; the concept of receiving input from human users, checking it for validity, and producing output for human users is well developed. However, the human user is only part of the equation. This Appendix discusses the other software users who also submit input and receive output but which are less understood and sometimes forgotten altogether by both developers and testers. There is a price to pay for ignoring these "invisible" users. The first step in proper accounting of these users is to understand their nature and how they can cause software applications to fail.

Key words: defensive programming, input validation, return values, software failure, system inputs

Introduction

Software is deterministic; given a starting state and a fixed series of inputs, the output produced by the software will be exactly the same every single time those inputs are applied. In fact, many of the technologies we apply during development (reviews, formal proofs, testing, and so forth) rely on this determinism, and would not work without it [2].

If software really is deterministic, then why do weird things always seem to happen? Why is it that we can apply a sequence of inputs and observe a failure and then be unable to reproduce that failure? Why does software work on one machine and fail on another? How is it that you can return from lunch and find that your Web browser has crashed when it wasn't being used?

The answer is, of course, that modern software processes an enormous number of inputs, and only a small percentage of these inputs originate from human users. Thus when testers can't reproduce failures, the reason is that they are only resubmitting human input, without regard to the operating-system return codes and input from runtime libraries. When software fails on a new computer after running successfully on another, the reason can only be that the new system is supplying input that differs in content from the old one, and the browser that crashes when you are at lunch is responding to input from a nonhuman external resource.

Testers and developers routinely ignore these invisible users, or even worse, do not realize they exist. But it is the mishandling of their inputs that causes hard-to-diagnose periodic system failure [4] and, worse, opportunities for hackers who are all too familiar with such weaknesses in software development practices.

The inputs from a software's environment—the operating system kernel, runtime libraries and external APIs, and the file system—are, in every way, the same as inputs from a human user; there are lots of them, many are invalid or produce error codes, and all of them should be validated before being processed by application software. The danger in not doing so is the same risk we take when we allow human users to enter input that is not validated: corrupted data, buffer overruns, and invalid computation results [3].

To demonstrate input from invisible users, we constructed a software tool that watches Windows programs while they run and identifies events that cross external interfaces. We then executed a number of applications and let our tool log all of the activity across their various interfaces. The results are eye opening. For example, Microsoft PowerPoint®, a complex and large application for making presentations and slide shows makes 59 calls to 29 different functions (excluding GetTickCount, which was called nearly 700 times) of the Windows kernel upon invocation. That means that a single input from a human user (invoking the application) caused a flurry of undercover communication to be transferred to and from the operating-system kernel.

Certainly, invocation is a special input and requires a great deal of setup and data initialization, but other operations are also demanding on low-level resources: when PowerPoint opens a file, 12 kernel functions are called a grand total of 73 times (once again excluding GetTickCount, which was called more than 500 times); when PowerPoint changes a font, 2 kernel functions are called a total of 10 times.

And these are only calls to the operating system kernel. PowerPoint also uses a number of other external resources (dynamically linked libraries), including mso9.dll, gdi32.dll, user32.dll, advapi32.dll, comctl32.dll, and ole32.dll, in the same manner as it uses the kernel. It is easy to see that the amount of communication between an application and its "invisible" users dwarfs visible human input.

Perhaps many of the mysterious and hard-to-reproduce system anomalies could be accounted for if we treated invisible users in the same way as we treat human users. If any of those calls produce unexpected return codes, then the system in question will have to handle these events and react appropriately.

To test applications' capabilities to handle such unexpected input, we perturbed some of these inputs so that the application in question received legitimate but unexpected return codes and data from its environment. For example, when an application allocates memory, we pass back an unsuccessful return code, or when the application opens a file, we tell it that there are no more file handles, and so forth. Every single application we tested in this manner failed within seconds (see the Typical Reactions to Low Memory Situations sidebar). The diagnosis: many software applications are unaware of the diversity and complexity of their environment. The expectation seems to be that nothing will go wrong, networks won't get congested, memory will never run out, and virus writers are just pranksters who can cause no real harm.[1]

Typical Reactions to Low-Memory Situations

We wrote a tool to simulate low-memory behavior and tested a number of standard industry applications. All the applications failed to gracefully handle unexpected return values from the kernel. Here are some of the results:

- *Scenario 1.* We loaded a legitimate page in a Web browser and then denied further attempts to allocate global and local memory. Then we reloaded the same page using the browser's Reload button. The browser returned an Invalid Syntax error message. Diagnosis: the syntax is obviously fine, because we reloaded a previously displayed page; however, the developer wrote a global exception handler, and the only thing he or she could think of that would cause the exception to be raised was that the user typed an invalid URL.

- *Scenario 2.* We selected the Open File dialog from a desktop application's menu and pointed it to a directory with lots of files. The files were listed correctly in the dialog box. Then we blocked access to local and virtual memory and redisplayed the same dialog box. The files were not listed (even though they still resided in the same directory). Diagnosis: not enough memory was available to correctly populate the Open File dialog box's display area, but the application had no facility to handle this situation. However, because we did not block access to creating the dialog-box window, the function completed without listing any files.

In scenario 1, the developer realized that the function might fail but did not fully consider all the ways it could fail. Thus we received an error message that did not describe the real problem and that was useless for diagnosing the failure. In scenario 2, the developer didn't even consider failure. The function completed as though it were successful, so the user was left wondering what might have happened to the files.

---

[1] See [1] for another case study detailing the failure of applications to handle failed system calls.

How important is it to handle these situations? Certainly, skeptics will argue that most of the time these inputs come in as expected, so that the cost of checking them (see the Validating User Input sidebar) is not money well spent. However, hackers are not so forgiving of the weaknesses of our software. Common attacks, such as packet storms to overwhelm memory and stress computing resources, are among a number of ways to cause denial of service by exploiting an application's lack of attention to its environment. Logic bombs are often triggered by external events such as a specific time (which is a return value of a kernel call and, therefore, an input) or other external events. How can we possibly test for such things without treating memory and system-call return values as inputs?

This is indeed the bottom line for software developers and testers: every single input from every external resource must be considered in order to have confidence in your software's ability to gracefully and safely handle malicious attacks and unanticipated operating environments. Deciding which inputs to trust and which to validate is a constant balancing act for developers.

FIGURE B.1 The execution environment for application software.

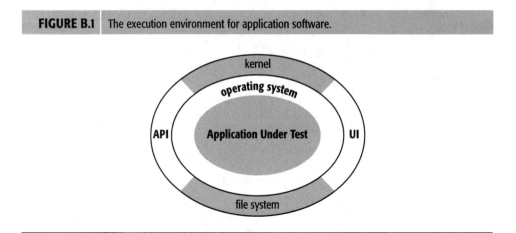

Where do these inputs come from? How do developers and testers need to handle them? Figure B.1 depicts a typical software application and its operating environment. The inner circle represents the application in question. Note that the boundaries of the application are completely contained within the operating system. Indeed, modern software communicates with nothing except the operating system, and all communication with any other external resource must go through the operating system first.

Beyond the operating system lie four classes of users (that is, any external resource with which software can communicate). These are human users, operating system users, API users, and file-system users. Each of these users, the types of inputs they can apply, and the challenges of dealing with them are discussed in the following sections.

The Human User

Here's a little fact that our human users often do not understand: their input does not actually touch the applications they use. However, programmers must understand this or risk inheriting bugs from the programs that really *do* process human input.

Consider keyboard input, for example. Keystrokes are interpreted first by a keyboard device driver, then passed through layers of operating-system libraries and APIs, and finally an event is generated and passed to the target application. The event is all the application sees; the many layers of operating-system libraries take care of interpreting the inputs from the human and translating them into something the application can deal with.

Can things go wrong with this process? Of course; software is involved, after all. Bugs in the operating system or code for GUI controls can cause all kinds of problems for an application expecting only a successful event. For example, what happens when you put too many entries in a list box? The list box will fill up and then either crash, in which case your application goes with it, or generate an error code that gets passed back to your application. If your application is not equipped to handle the error then it will crash—all on its own this time. It is imperative that programmers understand this process and learn which interface controls and APIs are trustworthy and exactly how and when they return error codes when they fail.

When developers do not handle GUI control error codes, they are risking denial-of-service attacks, which exploit such holes by finding ways to force the interface error to occur. Even worse, developers might explicitly trust data passed from a GUI control, which opens the door for potential buffer overruns when the user supplies enough data to fill up input buffers. Interface controls should not be trusted, and their input must be carefully constrained.

Compounding this situation are applications that allow developers to be users by exposing functionality that can be called from another program. In this case, two considerations must be taken into account:

1. Has the calling program supplied valid and meaningful parameters? Obviously, developers should check parameter validity just as they would check variable input through a GUI control.

2. Are there side effects to calls that preclude other calls from being executed properly? One common shortcoming is making the same call twice in a row.

The first call might open a file, and the software then expects the file to be read, not reopened, so the second call causes the software to fail. Because there is no GUI to conveniently protect the application from such invalid inputs, developers must be responsible for it.

Human users, whether the typical variety using an application through a GUI or developers using an application through a programmable interface, pose special but familiar problems to software developers and testers. But other types of users are not so familiar, and our handling of them can ensure the robustness of our applications or make them vulnerable.

Validating User Input

The most straightforward way to validate user input is to follow the Get Input command with a selection statement (*if, case,* and so on) that checks validity before continuing. But you must then encapsulate the input routines in a separate module to avoid littering the body of the code with *if*s. Remember, too, that all this checking will slow down your code. If the input is to be immediately stored, it is prudent to hide the storage structure behind a firewall of access routines (that is, make it an object). The access routines are then responsible for not allowing bad data into the structure. A popular, though unsafe, option is to simply raise an exception, trapping any errors. Beware of the side effects of exception handling, though. Programs tend to lose state information when exceptions occur because the instruction pointer has changed abruptly. When the instruction pointer is restored after the error routine executes, files could still be open and data might or might not be initialized, creating traps for unwary programmers. Preventing the input from ever getting to the application in the first place is possible only at the human user interface. GUIs are specifically designed to do just that. Specialized controls that will only allow integers (or other data types or formats) to be typed are a good way to filter unwanted input without having to write error routines.

The Operating-System User

The operating system is the only entity that interacts directly with application software. As discussed earlier, it is the intermediary between all physical users and application software; it also interacts directly with an application by supplying memory, file handles, heap space, etc. This latter part of the operating system is referred to as the kernel.

The Windows kernel, for example, exports over 800 different functions, each of which has at least two return values (for success and error conditions). This is indeed a challenge for developers, who all too often trust the kernel explicitly. When they allocate memory, they expect memory, not a return code saying "Sorry, it's all gone." Every time memory is allocated, the program has to check the return code for success before continuing its task. If it does not, then it will behave unexpectedly (or perhaps fail) when low-memory conditions actually occur.

The experiment cited in the Typical Reactions to Low-Memory Situations sidebar provide good evidence that developers put too much trust in their system calls always behaving as expected. Certainly this trust is often well-founded, but when an operating system is suffering a malicious attack such as a packet storm, it cannot and *should* not be trusted. But most applications either go blissfully unaware of such problems or they react by failing. If an application is to work safely and securely, it should not trust the operating system.

The API User

Like the operating-system user, APIs are external libraries that can be used to store data and perform various tasks for an application; for example, an application can make SQL queries to an external relational database or use APIs for programming sockets, performing matrix algebra, manipulating strings, and any number of other commonly reused functions.

These functions most often provide reliable service; however, they are also software and may contain bugs that must be considered when they are reused. They can also provide unsuccessful return values that must be handled properly; for example, a database could be off-line or contain corrupted data, or a socket connection could drop packets or fail to acknowledge a transmission because of network congestion. Developers must be aware of the possibilities, and testers must develop ways to test for them.

Trusting other software components leaves our own programs vulnerable to their bugs; and not fully understanding how the components behave when they fail subjects our software to unexpected, but legitimate, return codes.

The File-System User

Files, binary or text, are users and their contents are inputs, and, like the inputs we have already discussed, they could also be invalid. Files, even binary ones, are easy to change outside the confines of the applications that create and process them. What happens, for example, when a privileged user changes the permissions on a file that is being edited by another user?

An application's defenses against corrupted files are usually weak [5]. As long as the file extension is correct, the "magic string" is in place at the top of the file as an identifier, and the field delimiters are in place, then the contents are often read without being checked.

The dangers posed by this problem cannot be overstated. Reading files without validating content means that unknown data is being introduced to your software to be used for internal computation and storage. Data is the lifeblood of software, and when it is corrupt, the software is as good as dead.

Conclusion

Software applications are controlled by their environment. Unless every single input from every single user is checked for validity, the software can fail. But such overzealous defensive programming is probably not feasible for most software vendors. Indeed, given our experience cited earlier, it isn't likely that many vendors are aware of the extent to which their applications are dependent on "invisible" users of their software. Still, some precautions seem to be in order:

- During software design, we must continually recognize that users often go outside the boundaries of an application to get input from other users—and not just the human variety. Developers must understand that, ultimately, all users are software, that *users can be buggy,* and that their input must not be implicitly trusted. Deciding which inputs to verify and which inputs to trust should be done with full knowledge of the consequences.

- Testers must accept the challenge to simulate as many anomalous inputs as possible that are realizable and pose a threat to the application and the system on which it operates. This will mean new tools, new techniques, and purposeful consideration of *all* software users, even the ones we can't see.

- For systems that execute in a networked environment or protect sensitive data, understanding invisible users is as important as understanding human users. Software beware; you never know with whom you are communicating.

References

1.   A. Ghosh, "An Approach to Testing COTS Software for Robustness to Operating System Exceptions and Errors," *Proceedings of the International Symposium on Software Reliability Engineering.* Boca Raton, FL: 1999.

2.   R. Linger, H. Mills, and B. Witt, *Structured Programming: Theory and Practice.* Reading, MA.: Addison-Wesley, 1979.

3.   B. Miller, L. Fredrikson, and B. So, "An Empirical Study of the Reliability of UNIX Utilities," *Communications of the ACM,* Vol. 33, No. 12, December 1990. pp. 32–44.

4.   J. Richter, *Programming Applications for Microsoft Windows.* Seattle: Microsoft Press, 1997.

5.   J. Voas and G. McGraw, *Software Fault Injection: Inoculating Programs Against Errors.* New York: Wiley, 1998.

GLOSSARY
Annotated Glossary of Terms

001100101101101100001 100

API (Application Programming Interface) Software has two major interfaces. GUIs allow software to communicate with humans, and APIs allow software to communicate with other software. If your software has an API, people can write programs that can use your software directly. APIs are comprised of a number of functions and procedures that perform various tasks. Although this makes using your application easier, it presents another interface that you have to test for security vulnerabilities. Testing an API means writing programs that exercise the functions in the API.

Buffer Overflow A buffer overflow occurs when a program or process tries to store more data in a temporary storage area than there is space allocated for that data. The result is that the extra data "overflows" into some other storage area, overwriting what was there previously. This can be a severe security problem if this data overwrites an application's *instruction pointer*, the memory address of the next instruction the application will execute. Some languages, like C and C++, allow this to happen if application developers fail to constrain the length of input data. Buffer overflows account for nearly 80% of the security vulnerabilities reported in software.

Buffer Overrun *See Buffer Overflow.*

CERT® Coordination Center A major reporting center for Internet security problems. Staff members provide technical advice and coordinate responses to security compromises, identify trends in intruder activity, work with other security experts to identify solutions to security problems, and disseminate information to the broader community. They are most well known for their *CERT Advisories,* which alert users to newly discovered security vulnerabilities and threats.

Character Set Computers use binary numbers (1's and 0's) to represent character data, so each character is represented by a string of 1's and 0's. In fact, every number, character, special character, and control character has a unique sequence of 1's and 0's. When you type the character *f,* for example, the computer actually sees and reads the binary number that corresponds to that character. The ASCII character set is an example of such a character encoding. ASCII (the American Standard Code for Information Interchange) was designed with only the English language in mind. It uses only one byte (eight bits, or a string of eight zeros and ones). Multibyte character encodings are necessary to represent all the possible characters of more complicated languages, such as Japanese or Arabic. Perhaps the most popular multibyte encoding is UNICODE.

Computation Software computes as a result of simple mathematical expressions such as c=a+b. Software can compute using numbers, or it can compute by concatenating strings. Software computes things all the time, even when it is not directly solving a math problem. Whether it is fitting text into a display area, calculating how long a user has been on-line, or adding new elements to a list, computation is something that all software does on a regular basis.

Control Structure Computer programs are executed line by line from the beginning of a program to its end. A control structure allows programmers to change this sequence of instructions, allowing a program to branch out of sequence to another instruction. There are two types of control structures: *Branching* structures, such as the *if-then-else* statement, allow conditional execution of certain lines of code. For example, if a user enters a social security number, the programmer will often use a branching control structure to execute either error code (if the number is incorrect) or execute whatever code processes the number (if that the number is correct). *Looping* structures, like the *while* loop and the *for* loop, allow blocks of statements to be executed over and over. Developers might use a *while* loop to read a file. In other words, the loop would execute code that reads a single line of the file over and over until the end of the file is reached.

Controls *See User Interface Controls.*

Data Data is information stored by a program. Data comes in as inputs from users and is stored internally in what's called *data structures.* Explaining data structures thoroughly would take an entire book, but the most simple data structures are *integers* and *characters,* which store whole numbers and alphanumeric characters, respectively. More complex structures allow groups of numbers and characters to be stored. Common data structures are floating-point numbers, arrays, strings, lists, stacks, queues, and pointers (which only point to other structures). Any particular data structure can be *global,* which means that any program can access it, or *local,* which means that only the program that defines it can use it.

Data Structures *See Data.*

Debuggers Debuggers allow testers to take a low-level look at the application during execution. Hackers routinely employ debuggers to learn more about the target application and these tools are involved in any serious attempt to subvert application anti-piracy techniques.

Delimiters and **Fields** (in a data file) Information stored in a file isn't simply written to the file in a jumble of bits; if it were, it would be very difficult to read it back. An address book has *fields* for name, address, zip code, and so forth, so that if the address book is properly formatted, it is easy to quickly glance at the book to find a phone number, because you know exactly where to look (i.e., which field the number is stored in). Address books are formatted for easy reading by a human; files are formatted for easy reading by a program. Just as humans see the lines that separate fields in an address book, computers need to be able to see, for example, where the name field ends and the address field begins. Thus developers use symbols called *delimiters* to accomplish this; spaces, commas, semicolons, and the like are popular delimiters. Thus you might hear the phrase "a comma-delimited file" and imagine a line in the file would look something like this: Thompson, 150 West University, Melbourne, FL. A program can then be written to read the characters until the first comma and interpret that as the name, read the characters to the second comma and interpret that as the address, and so on.

Disassemblers Disassemblers are used to translate the machine code of binaries into their assembly equivalents. This allows attackers to browse through the executable's instructions in a human readable form to help them learn about the application. Sophisticated disassemblers and decompilers are used on the static program along with debuggers on the running application to reverse engineer the application.

Environmental Fault Injection Environmental fault injection is the process of simulating failures in the application's environment, for example depriving the application of disk space or prohibiting an external library from loading. Chapter 2 concentrates on environmental fault injection and many of the attacks there use Holodeck, a testing tool we created to fault-inject an application's environment at runtime.

Exception Sometimes errors occur that software is not programmed to prevent, either purposefully or inadvertently; when this occurs, an exception is raised. Normally, programmers write code called *exception handlers* that attempt to handle these situations; for example, suppose your application tries to insert data into a data structure that is already full of data. A "data out of bounds" exception may be raised by the runtime environment. If an exception handler is in place to handle this error, then the exception handler will be called. If the developers failed to include exception-handling code for such an error, then the application will crash (which in reality means that the OS shuts it down).

Fault Injection (of an application's environment) *See Environmental Fault Injection.*

Fault Model A fault model is a way of conceptualizing how software works so that you can better understand how it may fail. For the fault models used in this book see Chapter 1.

Fields (in a data file) *See* **Delimiters** and **Fields.**

Files Files are used to store *persistent* data. Files are better than data structures, because they constitute permanent storage. Data structures only "live" while the program that defined them is running. Thus all data that must be kept between executions of the software must be stored in files in order to be available the next time the application executes. Files are generally of two types: *Text* files are files stored in native text format, meaning that they can be read by a text editor and understood by humans. *Binary* files are stored in binary format, a format that is only machine readable.

Harness *See Test Harness.*

Hooks (for testing) *See Test Instrumentation.*

Input An input is an event that is generated outside an application that the application must react to in some fashion. Inputs can be keystrokes and mouse clicks, API calls, return codes, etc.

Instrumentation *See Test Instrumentation.*

Interface Software has many interfaces. The GUI (Graphical User Interface) is the most common, and represents the interface between the application and its human users. The API is an interface that an application exposes to other programs. Suppose you write a set of programs to perform math operations. As a developer, you would write some programs that would enable your application do its work. If you wanted any of these programs to be used by other third-party developers, you would write your code in such a way to allow these functions to be called by third-party applications. This is called *exposing,* or *exporting,* an interface; that is, you are allowing other programs to make programmatic calls into your application. Of course, because you can export your software to other applications, you can also *import* the interfaces of appropriately developed software, so that you can access *their* internal functions. To illustrate, think about how Microsoft Office® Excel® exports its interface to worksheet functionality, so that Word® users can embed worksheets into a word-processing document. Thus Word® can import the interface to Excel without the user realizing that Excel is even being used.

Memory Leak Programs often request memory to be allocated for their use (*see System Call*). Whenever memory is allocated, it should be freed (returned to the OS) when it is no longer needed. A *memory leak* is a bug in which memory is allocated but never freed; eventually, this bug will result in no more memory being available. Good commercial tools exist to help testers detect memory leaks.

Oracle Whenever tests are run, testers must verify that the outputs generated by the program were the outputs that were expected. Indeed, what good are tests that reveal bugs if the bugs go unnoticed by testers? Therefore, testers must establish a mechanism that is capable of comparing the actual output that the application under test produces with the expected output; this mechanism is called an *oracle*. Building an oracle is difficult, and general-purpose oracles remain one of the biggest unsolved problems in software testing.

Output An output is an event generated by an application that is sent outside the application for further processing. An output can be a message printed on the screen, a string sent to a database, a request sent to the operating system, etc.

Paging This term comes from computer architecture and is at the heart of the difference between *memory* and *storage*. Both memory and storage can contain data that can be read by programs. Storage means permanence: hard drives, floppy drives, and CD-ROMs are storage. If you turn off these mechanisms and turn them back on, the data will still be there. Memory, on the other hand, is temporary; each time you reboot your computer, memory is wiped clean. Although memory is temporary, it is much faster than storage—much, *much* faster. Thus when reading from a hard drive, the operating system will move more data into memory than is needed in order to speed up future data access. Paging is a term used to denote data being moved into or out of memory. You might hear the term *paged-in*, which means that the data in question has been moved into memory, because it is either needed by a program or might be needed soon. You might hear the term *paged-out*, which means that the data in question has been in memory longer than it is likely to be useful and has thus been paged out to make room for newer data.

Piracy Piracy, as used in this book, refers to the unauthorized duplication of software or copyrighted material (such as media files). Piracy is a serious and costly security concern for the software industry and digital media content providers.

Reverse Engineering (software) Reverse engineering is the art of examining an application in low-level detail to see how it works in order to duplicate or enhance that application. Although reverse engineering has legitimate uses in the software industry, there are strict laws against reverse engineering most commercial software.

Script kiddie A script kiddie is a person who is not technologically sophisticated who uses existing and usually well-known techniques, programs, or scripts to search for and exploit weaknesses in other computers on the Internet. These are not the people who initially find a security vulnerability but instead use applications developed by sophisticated hackers to exploit known vulnerabilities.

SQL *See Structured Query Language.*

SQL Injection SQL injection is an attack technique where SQL commands are entered into an input field or crafted as part of a string to try and force the application to execute commands on a database of an attacker's choosing. For more information on SQL injection and some examples read the sidebar "SQL Injection" in Chapter 3.

Structured Query Language (SQL) SQL is an ANSI (American National Standards Institute) language for accessing data from a relational database.

System Call *See also API.* A system call is a request for services made by a program to the operating system. Programs request such services as reserving memory to store data, establishing pointers to files, requesting date and time, etc. These requests of the operating system are collectively called *system calls.*

System Input Software receives many inputs from many different sources. One such source is the local operating system. When system calls *(see system call above)* are made by a program, the answer to the request comes back to the program as an input. These inputs are called *system input.*

Test Harness "Test harness" is a generic term that refers to a software tool that automates the testing process by running suites of test cases. Some test harnesses are created to do all the low-level interfacing with the application under test. Testers can then write test cases in higher-level scripting languages, which are interpreted by the harness to execute the tests.

Test Instrumentation In this book, we use "test instrumentation" to mean APIs that are included in the application for testing purposes. Many times, test instrumentation is added to allow *test harnesses* to easily access parts of the application under test.

Test Verification *See Oracle.*

User Interface Controls Human users communicate with applications via graphical user interfaces (GUIs). Applications receive input from humans through *controls* designed for the specific type of input being supplied. For example, if you want to enter text into a program, the program will present a control called a *text box* that is designed to receive such information. If you simply want to tell a program to process text you've already entered, then *button controls* that simply accept mouse clicks would be the appropriate choice. There are far too many GUI controls to describe here, but common ones are buttons, text boxes, list boxes, captions, spins, and drop-downs .

Index

DLLs (Dynamic Link Libraries). *See also* libraries
  Advapi32.dll, 164
  described, 19, 88
  Gdi32.dll, 164
  Mso9.dll, 20, 23, 164
  msrating.dll and, 2
  Ole32.dll, 164
  System32 directory and, 89
  User32.dll, 164
.doc file format, 141. *See also* Word (Microsoft)
documentation, 62
DVDs (digital video discs), 111
Dynamic Link Libraries. *See* DLLs (dynamic link libraries); libraries

E
e-commerce, 35
e-mail. *See also* Outlook Web Access (Microsoft Exchange Server)
  corrupt e-mail messages and, 33
  Eudora and, 31, 33
  implementation attacks, 101
  Mozilla and, 127
  Pine and, 101
  protocols, 127
embedded code, 3, 74. *See also* bugs
encryption, 9, 113, 128
engineering, reverse, 10, 175
environmental fault injection, 17–18, 159–162, 173
ERD (Emergency Repair Disk), 100
escape characters, 46, 47–56, 121, 134–135, 144
Ethereal Web site, 136
Eudora. *See also* e-mail
  corrupt e-mail messages and, 33
  described, 31
exceptions
  described, 173
  libraries and, 19
  unhandled, 19
Explorer (Windows), 77–78
extensibility, 112
external APIs, 164. *See also* APIs (Application Programming Interfaces)
external libraries, 112. *See also* libraries

F
failures
  bad data and, 31
  data corruption and, 31
  dependencies and, 19
  file names and, 30
fault injection, environmental, 17–18, 159–162, 173
fault model
  character sets and, 51–56
  described, 3, 5–7, 173
  general security concerns and, 7
  user-interface attacks and, 51–56
features taskbar, 110–111
fields, 30, 73

file(s). *See also* data; file formats; file names; file systems
  associations, 24
  configuration, 24, 131, 142
  corrupt, 30–33, 116–117, 130–131, 142–143
  delimiters, 121
  manipulating/replacing, 34–35, 117, 130–131, 143
  swap, 36, 118
  temporary, 37, 118, 125, 139, 146
file formats
  CDA, 120
  AIFF, 111
  AU, 111
  basic description of, 111
  DOC, 141
  MP3, 111, 117
  NSC, 119
  WAV, 111
file name(s). *See also* file formats
  common failures and, 30
  extensions, 111, 117
  implementation attacks and, 88–92, 124, 138–139, 146
  long file, 31
  problems related to, 30
file systems
  described, 17
  execution environments and, 166
  invisible users and, 169
  role of, in fault models, 7, 8
  software environments and, 164
File Transfer Protocol (FTP), 135
Folder.htt
  implementation attacks and, 91
  scripts and, 92
Form Manager (Mozilla), 127
FTP (File Transfer Protocol), 135
functionality, 78, 109

G
Gdi32.dll, 164
Get Input command, 168
GET method (HTTP)
  headers and, 50
  SQL and, 49
GetClickCount call, 164
GUI (Graphical User Interface). *See also* user interfaces; user-interface attacks
  buffer overflows and, 119
  controls, 167
  design attacks and, 62, 75
  input fields and, 30
  Mozilla and, 132
  OpenOffice.org and, 140
  remote users and, 146

H
hard disk(s)
  faults, 160–161
  space, 35, 118, 131, 143, 161

Internet Options dialog box, 44–45
IP (Internet Protocol) addresses, 71, 120
IRC (Internet Relay Chat), 126

J
JavaScript. *See also* scripts
    client-side scripts and, 49
    loop conditions and, 137
    Mozilla and, 126, 137
    skins and, 121

K
KB article bug, 28
Kerberos, 85
kernel, 7, 8, 164, 166

L
legacy systems, 62, 133
libraries. *See also* DLLs (Dynamic Link
        Libraries)
    access to, 19–23, 114–115, 129, 142
    external, 112
    Holodeck and, 20–23, 66
    media, in Windows Media Player, 112
    runtime, 164
    version numbers for, 24
licensed media, 111, 113, 117
links, hard, 143, 146
Linux. *See also* Linux OpenOffice.org
    configuration files and, 142
    e-mail and, 101
    hard links and, 143, 146
    OpenOffice.org and, 139
    port scanners and, 145
    SAMBA and, 96–97
    Slackware, 140
Linux OpenOffice.org
    configuration files and, 142
    dependency attacks and, 142–143
    described, 107, 139–140
    design attacks and, 144–146
    implementation attacks and, 146–147
    intelligent automation and, 142–143
    macro features and, 140–142, 144
    planning your attacks and, 139–147
    port scanners and, 145
    source code and, 108
    user-interface attacks and, 144
    Web site, 141
LoadLibrary function, 20, 22
LoadLibraryExW function, 20, 21, 23
logging, remote, 37
long
    file names, 31
    string attacks, 144
loop conditions
    denial of service and, 73
    design attacks and, 73–74, 122–123, 137,
        145
    user-supplied logic and, 73
LPT1 port, 89

M
macros
    design attacks and, 74
    OpenOffice.org and, 140–142, 144
manual control slider, 159
MAX_PATH value, 31
Media Guide (Windows Media Player), 110, 112
Media Library (Windows Media Player), 112
media players, 6–7. *See also* Media Player
        (Microsoft)
Media Player (Microsoft)
    dependency attacks and, 114–118
    described, 110
    design attacks and, 121–124
    features taskbar and, 110–111
    file types and, 111
    Holodeck and, 116
    implementation attacks and, 124–125
    IP addresses and, 120
    licensed media and, 117
    Media Guide, 110, 112
    Media Library, 112
    network interface, 113
    streaming media and, 112
    user-interface attacks and, 118–121
    version 9.0, 107, 110–125
    Web site, 112
memory
    faults, 162
    invalid URLs and, 165
    leaks, 174
    logic bombs, 166
    low, 118, 131, 143, 165–166
    scenarios, typical reactions to, 165
    stress testing, 118
Microsoft Active Server Pages (ASP), 48–49
Microsoft Developer Network (MSDN), 91
Microsoft Exchange Server. *See* Outlook Web
        Access (Microsoft Exchange Server)
Microsoft Internet Information Server (IIS), 44
Microsoft Internet Explorer browser
    Content Advisor, 20–23, 114
    Corrupt files and, 30
    design attacks, 68–70, 74, 77
    Holodeck and, 21
    Implementation attacks and, 89
    Internet Options dialog box, 44–45
    libraries and, 20–23
    loop conditions and, 74
    machine scans in, 68–70
    msrating.dll and, 23
    user-interface attacks and, 44–45
Microsoft Office, 139–140
Microsoft PerfMon, 38
Microsoft PowerPoint, 164
Microsoft Visual Basic Scripting Edition
        (VBScript)
    design attacks and, 74
    Server.HTMLencode and, 50
Microsoft Windows 3.1, 24
Microsoft Windows 95, 24

License Agreement

The software applications on the attached CD are research prototypes developed by faculty and students at Florida Tech and may contain copyrighted or patented code. It is offered "as is" for the purpose of reproducing the attacks published in this book and for experimentation by the reader on their own software products. The author and publisher make no warranties and accept no liabilities arising from use or misuse of the products.

By installing the applications on the CD, the reader accepts these terms.

CD Contents

Holodeck v 1.3 incorporates fault injection capabilities and advanced logging of interactions between the application and its environment for debugging and fault isolation. With it you can simulate environmental faults—such as low memory, network failure or write protected disks—to expose security vulnerabilities in your application.

Installer Details

The Holodeck installer is very much like a Windows Installer you would normally see from most commercial applications. It is very simple to follow and simply requires the execution of the "Setup.exe" file in the "Holodeck" directory.

For further information visit:

How to Break Software Security companion Website:
http://www.howtobreaksoftware.com/security

FITScanner v 1.0 is a simple, easy to use port scanner that you can use to assess your application's exposure to the network.

Installer Details

The FITScanner installer is similar to the Windows Installer you would normally see from most commercial applications. Launching the installer requires the execution of the "Setup.exe" file in the "FITScanner" directory.

For further information visit:

How to Break Software Security companion Website:
http://www.howtobreaksoftware.com/security

System Requirements for Holodeck and FITScanner

Operating System: Windows 2000 (Professional, Server, Advanced Server), Windows XP (Home, Professional), Windows Server 2003.

Pentium 200mHz w/ 64MB RAM (minimum); Pentium II 400mHz w/ 128MB RAM (recommended)

This software does NOT WORK on Windows NT or Windows 95/98/Me.

This book comes with a CD that contains two very useful testing tools that were written by faculty and students at Florida Tech.

In addition, *www.HowToBreakSoftware.com/security* is your online gateway to the latest tool updates, bug stories, security breaches, and technology related to the field of software security.